Practice of Satsang

PRACTICE OF SATSANG

PS: Conscious Living – Celebrating the Truth of Who You Are

NATASHA DALMIA

PARTRIDGE

A Penguin Random House Company

To order additional copies of this book, contact
Toll Free 800 101 2657 (Singapore)
Toll Free 1 800 81 7340 (Malaysia)
orders.singapore@partridgepublishing.com

www.partridgepublishing.com/singapore

CONTENTS

Peaceful Sacredness

Attributed to my Grandparents and Parents,
Hugs,
Nitu

Letters to my Grandchildren

Sautéed in Questions,
Spiced with Stories,
Drained out Assumptions,
Although residues remain,
Garnished with Quotes,
And
Simmered in Practices

By
Natasha Dalmia,
31 years old, writing to her future.

*May our hopes for future inspire us to practice consciously, mindfully now,
And be at peace with the past.*

Foreword by Jacqueline Wong

Warning!
All characters in this book are real.
If you find any semblance to any imaginary
character, it is purely coincidental.
:)

For everyone who is grateful for the wonder of life.

Gratitude to every conscious soul, trying and caring.
Gratitude to all who courageously allowed their story
to be shared and trusted me with it.
There is an ocean full of stories.
This book just has a few of those who have shaped me.

Grateful for every conscious offer to support
Editing Assistance: Sheshank Dalmia
Book Cover Design & Logo: Vinay Raja
Book Cover Illustration: Christina Awad
And for the blessings and love of many more, in visible and invisible ways

Conscious Lady of Oneness

Christina Awad

I am Lady of Oneness, your reflection
I am of Earth and Divine
I am of flesh and of imagination
The roots of your ancestors,

Awaken me through the feminine and the masculine
I bring you the sun, I bring you the moon
I am your mind, body & soul
I am your expression
The ruler of your inner world
The pilot of your outer world
I am your conscious and subconscious
The trigger of your thoughts
The gardener of your dreams
The orchestrator of your decisions
I plant your seeds,
I come here to guide you to your truth
I come to reveal YOU,

Come let us dance with the elements
Let us vibrate as one
For I am you and you are me

Grateful for inspiration, hope, peace and love

FOREWORD

Nurturing Communities of Truth and Consciousness

"We shape clay into a pot, but it is the emptiness inside
that holds whatever we want." Dao-de jing

As I reflect on the chapters and beautiful stories that fill the pages of Natasha's book, Practice of Satsang, I think about the work we share as colleagues at Sequoia Group where we seek to further the work and understanding of what it takes to co-create communities and organizations truly worthy of commitment.

A community is a place where we experience a sense of belonging - it means being at home, in the broadest sense of the phrase. The notion of being at home is a simple and yet profound way of describing our experience when we feel seen, heard and recognized, a place we can be truly ourselves and feel always welcomed. The opposite is to feel isolated, an outsider, or one who does not fit into the social norm, one who needs to be somehow cured. When we see the possibilities of the community, we start to see the people who enter into our lives as gifts, and not as people we have to be fixed or be made whole. Rather than parents as providers, children become our teachers and a powerful source of motivation for building a better life; rather than companies creating jobs for employees, we see that without the employees, there is no enterprise; and rather than governments ruling the citizens and creating townships, citizens create leaders and help to build self-sustaining communities where governments fail. Thich Nhat Hanh, the Zen Buddhist teacher once said that it is the essential nature that all things are interconnected, we "inter-are". Indeed, the nature of reciprocity or inter-being is one of the fundamental principles that under gird a vibrant and meaningful community.

If Satsang means "being with the truth", then I would consider my children as my best teachers in this regard. Growing up with them has taught me some of the most profound lessons on authenticity.

Since the time my elder son, Daniel started pre-school, we would have dinner time conversations, sacred connections we share with each other how our day went. The starter was a simple question "What was the best thing that happened today?" Sometimes, the conversation would bring us to laughter, and occasionally, to tears. But these were moments of connection that we cherished where we had a peek into each other's separate lives at school or at work. However, this tradition, like many other traditions, eventually grew banal as the years went by, even though we tried to keep up with it. One time, my husband and I thought perhaps it was time to stop when Daniel become a "tween" – a new word invented to describe the interesting gap years between being a child and a teenager, when we noticed he would often give single-word answers such as "Fine", "Great", "Tired" or "Awesome", in response to our question "How was your day?"

One day, I had a particularly difficult conversation with a client at work and could not shake the heavy-hearted feeling all through the day. This must have shown on my face when I turned up at the dining table. My son, nonchalantly asked "So mum, what was the best thing that happened today?" with a wink and the kindest of smiles. We all laughed heartily at his witty act and eventually talked about what was upsetting me, and I even found some solution to the difficulty that had eluded me before. He knew it was his turn to take lead when he knew I was not capable of doing so.

The stories in Nat's inspiring debut "Practice of Satsang", embodies this simple truth and essential principle of reciprocity. If words create worlds, the world she has written about as a series of letters to her future grandchildren interweaves poignant truth about life and questions that would invoke deeper curiosity rather than give easy answers. She calls us all to become seekers ourselves and to remember to appreciate the Source from which all life flows. This is a book that will continue to inspire generations to come.

With Gratitude to all our Grandmothers and Grandmothers-to-be,
Jacqueline

Jacqueline Wong
M.SC. POSITIVE ORGANISATION DEVELOPMENT
Director & Founder, Sequoia Group

INTRODUCTION

Practice of *Satsang* is an invitation for conscious living.

'Sat' means truth and *'Sanga'* means company. *Satsang* is an old Sanskrit word meaning, 'being with the truth', and 'gathering together to find the truth'. Usually, in my culture, it was interpreted to gather in the presence of a *guru* (teacher), who would help to be with the truth.

As I grew up, I realized there are many *gurus* (teachers) in our lives who help us to be with the truth, with our truth. They come in unexpected relationships and situations as our own higher consciousness or in the form of parents, siblings, friends, colleagues and strangers. The key is in my openness, perception and choice to reflect and remember. Am I willing to recognize the teacher, the truth and the times of *sangha* in my inner and outer worlds?

What if every moment, situation and person in our lives offers us the opportunity to see or be the *guru* in ourselves or in others?

I lived into this question and began to have new eyes for myself, and my old and new relationships. So, *Satsang* became a way of living for me, to be willing to see the *guru* in myself and in every person I meet and I am with. *Satsang* became a way of being for me, where I support others to remember the *gurus* in their own higher consciousness and also see it in that of others. *Satsang* became a practice for me.

My grandmother had introduced me to these Sanskrit words. I believe my first *guru* is my grandmother who would teach me invaluable lessons of life after school in our evening conversations. It was my special time where I could pester her with questions about life that was not part of the school curriculum, listen to the hymns she sang, understand the meaning behind the lyrics and wonder what God was up to!

My favourite was her creative story telling sessions, both fiction and non - fiction. Those stories helped me understand the truth about life, even if they changed from time to time, depending on her health, mood and circumstances. As I grew up, I realized the consistency in inconsistencies, as one responds to situations based on their consciousness and choice in the moment, akin to a living system. This is also the truth in the rich human tapestry of life. I recall once when she could not go to a 'real religious *satsang*' held in the town because of health reasons, she found solace in the story she made up that she was attending a *satsang* with me as we both turned to then audio *gurus* to listen to and learn from. Anything that one read, listened to or did to help raise consciousness and be a better person was a practice of *satsang*. She looked better even as she spoke. I was happy.

Sitting in a leadership workshop in Budapest in 2011, when I was stirred to reflect on my purpose of life, when I was wondering in all honesty what is it truly that I care about and wish to nurture in this lifetime, I suddenly knew.

With the awareness of my role as a helper in various forms; management consultant, executive coach, facilitator or teacher or friend, my practice and my relation to the field of transformation was shaped. I became committed to honour authenticity in all its darkness and light and to support people in their intentional transformative journeys, be it individual, familial, organizational or global. Trusting the higher consciousness of others and being with that truth alone is enough. Reminding them of it or co-creating safe spaces for emergence to occur became my work in which I witnessed the truth of love, light and life.

Questions arise about the world we are living in now, and the world we wish to live in or the world we wish for our children and grandchildren. Who will make the shift if not us, now?

Seeing many search for happiness, meaning and *gurus* in their lives today, despite the abundance and accessibility of knowledge and technology, we realize together that the secret lies in the inner worlds of our being. Often times, the password to that wealth within us are quiet, reflection time, unlocked by a question or story that matters. Sometimes, the presence of another to listen to the story, the wavering thoughts, and the extreme emotions without judgment is a gift both for the receiver and the giver. Through my work and play, I have had the opportunity to spend hours in conversations, swimming through oceans of questions and seas of stories shared by people across generations and cultures.

Each person is a story worth discovering. Each person is a guru for us if only we allow him or her to be. The question is, what do we choose to see/hear/feel for another, or not?

Each of those moments when the person is being with her/his truth, as hard as that might be is Practice of *Satsang*. Each of those moments when the person hopes to be better is Practice of *Satsang*. Each of those moments when the person is challenging one self and asking questions that matter to her/him is Practice of *Satsang*. Each of those moments when the person is trying with the first step is Practice of *Satsang*. Each of those moments when the person witnesses and acknowledges one's own collapse in the old patterns of thoughts and actions is Practice of *Satsang*. Each of those moments when the person is trying again and again authentically to be truthful to the self and to accept another's truth with love is Practice of *Satsang*.

I do not mean any religious group or person when I use this Sanskrit word of wisdom. I am not even an expert on *Satsang*. I am simply a soul traveler, sharing my questions, reflections and stories with you, trusting that you would share yours with the next soul traveler in your family, friendship, work or other circle. I believe *Satsang* to be this gathering in life on Earth to remember and be with our individual, collective and universal truth.

Practice of *Satsang* is celebrating the truth of who you are.

What is the ringing of Your bell?
What resonance are you tuning to?
What sound of music are you dancing to and playing for other people in your life?

Journey as you read this book, inwards to your own genius, wisdom, consciousness, bliss and truth. Notice as you read the questions what comes up for you in your life stories. Notice you are ever-expanding consciousness as you revisit and make meaning of any story of your life to be at peace with it. Notice the gift of your learning nature when awakened for yourself and others. Notice the impact of your life on others, and others' lives on yours.

As you read others' stories, and perchance, you happen to find any similarities, partly or remotely with any character or situation in any story, be with the connectedness. Know that you are not alone.

Know that yet, you are unique in your own story. Both the good and the not-so-good ones give us an opportunity to reflect, to act in a way that is conscientious. Through all our victories, mistakes, moments and truths of this human life with family, friends or fellow-travelers, colleagues, clients or communities, we can touch the true consciousness of our souls, again and again.

As you become the observer of your own life, thoughts and emotions, and practice peaceful sacredness in the ordinary moments in life, you may experience the Shangrila of stillness and pure happiness. You may see, touch and taste a personal truth, which per chance may be universal too. You may feel an expansion of consciousness which suddenly vanishes as you identify with the next thought or emotion or achievement. It is ok. You know that peace and happiness is available to you. It just needs practice and acceptance.

Written as Letters to my Grandchildren, when I do not even have children as of now, I invite you to join me in cherishing the present moment awareness seeing a future filled with hope, love, peace and joy. We can choose to feel that hope, love, peace and joy in the now, right now. I imagine if I practice enough now, I will be ready to share stories and my way of being as I hope to with my children and grandchildren, if and when the time comes.

Namaste,
Natasha

PART
1

Practice of *Satsang* with Family

An Anchor for my Life ~

~ Letters to my grandchildren ~

My dear little ones, out of the many words you will learn starting with the alphabet 'A', I have a few fundamental ones to share. In addition to 'Apple' or 'Aeroplane', words that helped me to understand the world, the outer world, I was curious to gain access to the mysterious inner world that exists within us. The secret to peace, happiness and fulfillment lies in there. Our inner world determines how we respond to the outer world - people, places and perspectives. Practicing the essence of the few fundamental words below has been life-giving, nourishing and key to expanding possibilities for me.

As you grow each day into beautiful beings, I invite you to experiment, play and discover the essence of these words in your life. As you master the game, you will get clues to master your life and create your own future that is meaningful, day-by-day. The key is to choose wisely and practice consciously. Remember, whatever you practice; consciously, sub-consciously, or unconsciously, right or wrong, it grows stronger. So, what do you choose?

A for 'Awareness'

- What do you practice to expand horizons of thoughts, emotions and actions, creating new awareness and learning for yourself and others?

A for 'Awe' and 'Appreciation'

- What are the small and big moments in life that you are grateful for, that fills you with awesome awe and makes you appreciate the very gift of life?
- What do you do to create such meaningful moments, re-framing your past, living your present and creating your future?

A for 'Allowing' and 'Accepting'

- What principles, values and circumstances do you accept in your life?
- What diversity and differences do you allow yourself to learn from?

Other words, also starting with 'A', also served me but only for short-term. Practice of the essence of these words fed my ego and exhausted me in the long-term as I found them to be life-depleting (Argh!);

A for 'Anger', 'Arrogance', and 'Argumentation'.

Practice of *Satsang* with Family – A Story

An Anchor for my Life ~

'Aek baar' ... aka ... 'Once upon a time' was a part of our daily thread of conversations at home. It was the key to unlock doors from memories, experiences and information. It was the secret passageway to stories shared with sweet and spicy tastes of the Indian cuisine. It was defining moments from whence I learnt much about life and culture.

Your great-great-grandparents (my grandparents) have narrated many a story to me. When I stitch the bits and pieces together, they form a lovely, colorful tapestry of our family history, geography, chemistry and maths! I probably began contributing my mini pieces that they weaved in masterfully, perhaps since the day I was born, or since the day I uttered my first intelligent word, *'ayeishhi'*, spitting some baby saliva in the attempt. (Well I bet it was intelligent to me – then!).

So, *aek baar*, a long time ago, when I was about one-and-a-half-years-old, my mother's father, my grandpa *(nanaji)*, took me to his home for a holiday when father was sick and mother was torn thin attending to the well-being of everyone but herself. He stays in a town few hours away from my parents called Siliguri (later on in life, I would liken it to the famous Malgudi or just call it Darjeeling, yes, from where the famous, delicious tea comes from, as they fell in the same district.)

I am told that I was a happy, easy-going, rather fun child. At least I only remember the positive characteristics that they described of me! I have three aunts, my mother's sisters, young and unmarried then, Sarita, Sunita and Babita, who took care of me and fussed over me. I became everyone's favourite toy and soon before anyone knew it, I just ended up growing in my grandparent's home. There was no strategic planning around it. There was no crisis or convenience. It was just, as my grandma calls it, the flow of life. My parents would visit me from time-to-time. It was all, just, natural. At that age

5

and stage of life, I must have been happy getting all that I needed and creating a hell-of-a-fuss if I did not.

By the time I turned three, it was time to tame me. I was enrolled in the best convent school of the town that my mother was an alumnus of. With the passage of time, each of my aunts got married. Soon enough, it was just my grandmother, *nanima*; grandfather, *nanaji* and I – two and a half people, as they fondly referred to us. Life was simple, then. My inner world and outer world were balanced. I would give free reign to my curiosity to explore my small outer world. Of course I only had the awareness and perspective of this later in life.

Your great-great-grandparents would be awake by 5:00 am every single day. Some days it would be as early as 3:30 - 4:00 am or as late as 6:00 am. I can make a guess of what you might be thinking that this sounds crazy, right? I thought so too!

I wondered as a child what they would do waking up that early. It was not like they had home-work to do, or prepare for those detestable tests or examinations, or debates, or elocutions, which was the real hard work in life. In their school days, they were allowed to play more than study – a stark opposite of my reality that I did not like one tiny bit.

One day I was determined to find out. I put three alarms and forced myself to wake that early. I tagged behind *nanima*. She washed the prayer utensils, while *nanaji* brought some milk. Then she made hot ginger masala *chai*, tea and they sipped it in silence or simple conversation. That's it! I was expecting something huge that would awe me.

As a seven-eight year old, I could not appreciate or even comprehend this routine. I felt it was utter wastage of precious time, when instead one could sleep blissfully and stay up late in the night prior to it. It was not logical but somehow, for many days, it was compelling enough for me to join them, even though I was not officially allowed to have the delicious tea till I was eighteen! (Are you sharing my sentiments as you read this? It is tea, not alcohol!)

It became a daily routine. I would hear *nanaji* calling my name and wishing me good morning, repeatedly. It was the best alarm clock when I would wake up to snooze the wishing, snuggle up and lay down on *nanima's* lap, who responding to the most natural instinct of a woman, would begin to caress my back. *Nanaji* would make funny faces at me, as if to convey, 'ahem – lucky you!' I would return a cheeky smile and get into a tighter ball, when after what seemed like just a minute, *nanima* would push me, 'time to get up and get ready for school!' I loved my school, although I would have been happier if it started only at mid-day and we could sleep some more in the mornings. Even so, I would proudly wear my St. Joseph's batch and get ready punctually each day. *Nanima* was first shocked, later bemused as I would join my hands in *namaste* to pray to Ganesha, Krishna, Shiva, Sarasvati etc. for good marks and then make a cross to appease Jesus too, every morning before I hurried off for school. It felt all natural to integrate, to accept, to follow a routine.

I had felt loved, secure and at home. ('At home' is another phrase that held much significance in my life only after I grew up and left home) It dawned upon me much later about the sacredness of the space created naturally by them. No TV or news was allowed in that space. There was no intrusion of the internet, as cyber space and mobiles did not exist then and even when it did in later years, it did not interrupt the practice of conversations over *chai*. It became an anchoring story for me in later years of life when amidst all insanity and stress in life, I would think of 'Home'. Irrespective of which time zone I was in, I knew that in one corner of the world at 5:00 am, hot ginger masala tea and stories are cooked every day by my two favourite people, even if the 'halfling' is away!

Out of the many stories, the one where *nanaji* had brought me home at one-and-a-half-years old was his favourite and oft-narrated tale by *nanima* through the decades. It used to amuse everyone how like a little monkey or duckling, I had imprinted on him. I used to beam up every time I saw *nanaji*, screaming fiercely in my childlike voice, 'he is MY grandfather' to all his daughters and my aunts, who would roll their eyes exasperatedly, muttering, 'Yes, we know that, surely, by now!' I did not understand sarcasm at that age. I was just happy that I was successful in warding off any claims. I had felt enough, complete.

Then one day after a decade, when the same story was re-told for the umpteenth time, it suddenly came to my awareness that my inner world had shifted, even though the outer world remained the same. I felt distant from my grandparents. The chill childhood days had turned to 'those teenage days'.

Nanima's wishes for me was to grow into an ideal lovely lady, get married and continue with the traditions and norms of our culture, just as she had done so, and her children had done so. However, I would see myself differently and was craving to do some-thing with my life. I just did not know what, or how. I would mercilessly argue with her about the roles and restrictions on women that our culture imposed. Other cultures seemed more freeing. If only I can become independent, I would be free. I would tell her of my plans and hopes to be independent. She had never heard of such bizarre thoughts from any generation so far and prayed for me. There was a storm brewing in my inner world. I did not feel loved or understood anymore and wanted to go far away from home. I felt adrift and alone having lost my anchor, my inner peace.

Nanaji, who was so carefree to smile and express affection, when I was a little child, seemed to have grown serious and withdrawn as I grew up. I silently gave him the nickname of angry old man, inspired by Bollywood's 'angry, young man' nickname for the famous Amitabh Bachchan. Work had become intense for *nanaji*. He worked hard as the sole bread provider for the family, even as he aged. He has been one of the best in his times. But times were changing. Yet, my grandparents followed the rules of age-old times. I could never understand the logic of why were men always the sole bread providers in 99% of the families in our culture, even though women were getting educated and ready to step up in business. Yet, the women were given no opportunities, strictly. Their educational qualifications only seemed to serve as a status in the matrimonial columns. Why were we made to stress to excel in the school when all that seemed to matter was the school of marriage?

I wondered if it were as confusing for boys too, growing up in our culture. What were their opportunities and challenges? What were the messages of past generations for them? What were we still accepting and allowing?

Some things that we studied in school as social evils were still accepted and allowed in our culture. For example, a girl's parents had many duties to perform. They were supposed to provide for the girl before and after marriage, in the form of dowry, gifts, this and that. Little wonder that it was considered to be lucky to have a boy, who would continue your lineage, look after you in your old age, attend to your funeral rites and offer prayers to your spirits after you were gone. Despite evidence on the contrary, where girls were stepping up, the cultural norms continued to have different preferences for boys and girls. But why such norms, I wondered as a teenager, when the world was changing and adults cannot determine or control the gender of an unborn child anyway? (Of course there were unfavourable means to control that tipped the balance of nature and led to far more complex social problems – which is another story altogether.)

Wishing that I were a boy, I would ask *nanaji* innumerable questions about work, business and career but I was given vague answers, underpinned by the fact that I was a girl and a child (even though I was a teenager; that is almost an adult, right?). Although done so with the best of intentions to protect me, the impact on me was unfavourable. I felt helpless when I was not allowed to manage his business, go to his meetings etc. He would tell me that there was no need and that he could manage it all. I did not doubt that one bit. After all, he had managed it all very well while raising four daughters, getting them educated, married etc. I was just keen to learn the practical side of business and work life from him as a teacher.

I was cautioned by *nanima* not to poke him with incessant questions. It was rude for a lady to ask questions. It was best to follow rules silently. It just left me aghast to know of the rules. Who made those rules in the first place? In agony, I re-directed my questions at her instead. I asked her point-blank if she was happy? She was, to my utter surprise. She taught me to see the positive in dire situations that one could not change. I wondered, with retaliation, why she would still feel that tinge of guilt and regret for not giving birth to a boy then.

Today, as I look back at my struggles in the identity that was desired of me and the identity that I wished to create for myself, I realize I carved and sharpened my core and strengths because of those very struggles. *Nanima* had inadvertently created a beautiful safe space by allowing me to spill my barricade of questions, in her not knowing, and in her unfailing efforts to keep the conversation going on with me. She told me firmly that even though we differed much in our viewpoints, behaviours, perspectives, we had one thing in common – we both wanted the best for me. *Nanaji* and I speak about business, working life today, and he does so with a glint of pride. I learnt the invaluable lesson of gauging the strength of a relationship by measuring the deeper underlying intentions that form the rock bed than the shifting behaviour shown up in events alone. I also learnt to allow time and space for change to happen as we continuously weave our life stories.

One day, in my early teenage years, I was told not to enter the prayer house or the kitchen! Why? What did I do now? *Nanima* worked alone in the kitchen and returned hours later. I immediately confronted her. She sighed and seemed to struggle to explain why, looking for logic because she knew I would ask for that. I prodded on, secure in the knowledge that *nanaji* was not at home. If he ever heard my loud defiant voice, he would mute it in a minute with his booming voice. I likened him to a lion in the savannah. In his absence, I pretended to be one. Perhaps at a sub-conscious level, the imprint continued.

Nanima looked at my young teenage self, shook her head and sat me down to explain the rites a woman should go through once she begins to menstruate and what that means in our culture. Why was it such a big deal, I wondered? I had learnt all of that in Biology, as something very practical and unavoidable. I became angry as I heard how women are perceived to be dirty during that period. They are not even allowed to go to the prayer room to worship! But my Christian friends go to church even when they are menstruating, I challenged *nanima*. I smiled wickedly, imagining hundreds of girls telling the nuns at school that they had their periods at the same time, only to skip mass!

Why are women considered dirty if they bled when the same blood is used to create a fetus? It frustrated me that *nanima* seemed to accept what I called the limiting thoughts and myths. She recalled her teenage days when girls were married (child marriage was legally prevalent then) even before they got their menstruation and enjoyed the break from the back-breaking housework. Perhaps those rules and myths came about then that were in the best interest for women. I guessed I understood somewhat. There are always stories of why certain rituals and norms are created in the first place that is justified. Except, who keeps a tab on them to see where they end up going, and in what shape and form? I felt exasperated by the stories. What was the logic for pickles to become sour and spoil if a menstruating woman touched it?

I still recall on another day, when I had forgotten and accidentally touched the big jar of freshly made pickles during my periods. I felt shame, fear and regret. Perhaps sub-consciously, I accepted the very limiting thoughts that I was questioning. I remember keeping an eye on that pickle jar for a month afterwards to see if it got spoilt. It did not, not even till its relishing end. What became sour, thankfully, was my belief in those myths. I told her of this episode after 15 years as we both broke down in giggles looking back at memories and behaviours that now seem so silly.

Listening to my interpretations of the memories, my changing emotions with age and time, my meaning-making of what were just simple life events after fifteen odd years, *nanima* was pleasantly surprised. Events and their stories, emotions and interpretations change with time. It is interesting to note that some times, we also get stuck in our own stories. Releasing them gratefully, appreciating the past fully is a freeing experience. We spent hours walking down memory lane, her past, my past, our past, pausing at the different pieces in the museum that evoked laughter, tears, new awareness and shared meaning making. We get a glimpse of the truth when we expand our awareness through the eyes of the other. She did not remember half the stories from which I had learnt life lessons, values she had taught me and was so shy when I expressed my gratitude. I had been a good student to her albeit an annoying one. As a student, it was priceless to remember the lessons and remind my teacher of her worth. I was surprised that she was surprised by that. She has forgotten her priceless contributions.

She told me how I had been a teacher to her too with my undying questions that made her reflect. She had made mini changes and broken 'rules' like Not throwing the auspicious materials after Hindu Pujas into our local Mahananda river, when I would rant, 'How we are polluting our rivers!'. Initially, she would state how it does not make a difference if one family alone breaks the rules. I would agree but did not know how to convince all families. So sometimes, we would be the first one to change trusting that gradually desired change at a larger scale will happen. We found win-win solutions in many other situations. New awareness revived and rejuvenated our relationship. Our thoughts might have been at different polarities and at war with each other, but the center was the deepening relationship that was constantly evolving.

Even as a young child, I often wondered what might I teach and learn from my children and grandchildren in the far future. I wonder if I will be alive to co-create safe story-telling and learning spaces with you. I do encourage you to create them though.

In the human skin, perception is reality. Reality creates perception. My parents and grandparents had faced new challenges in bringing me up, for the first time ever in their generation. They did not have the answers to my questions. Their past had not equipped them to deal with my present and questions for my future. But their present and their presence in bringing me up helped us all to prepare for the future. They blessed me that hopefully I would teach the new answers to the new generations. They were aware that the realities of the coming generations were changing at a larger scale than it ever had and wanted me to be ready to sail with the winds of change.

My resentment towards my family changed as I outgrew my teenage years. I began to see opportunities instead and felt secure again. Life is akin to high and low tides. I realized that I felt ready to sail when I was given the freedom to pursue my thread of questions, curiosity, discoveries through studies and career. And I felt truly free when even in my search for independence, having left my shore, I was anchored in my relationships back home that had survived storms, lightning, hail, hell's fire, boredom and much more, both in the inner and outer worlds.

I hope and pray for you that you feel anchored in your inner world and in your relationships in life. I trust you to practice the gift of appreciation, of being in touch with your true essence in both good and bad times for yourself and for others.

Yours lovingly,

Grandma

PS: So, my lovely grandchildren, what are your stories as you notice your growth in your awareness of appreciating, allowing, accepting and inevitably making choices, as your *Practice of Satsang*, in your times?

(Invite you to write or share YOUR story that is bubbling within you ...)

"I can help you if you are blind. But I cannot help you if you close your eyes tightly and pretend to be blind! Yet, I am waiting for you to open them."

-Shakuntala Chaudhary (2013)
-(*Nanima*, Homemaker)

"Face your truth and learn to accept it. Do not run away from it. That is life."

-Prem Lal Chaudhary (2013)
-(*Nanaji*, Businessman)

Now, it is time for Practice.
You may create your own or experiment with one I suggest below.

Practice
(A)

To be aware of your own patterns of thinking. Awareness is the first step for change, even if awareness feels like you have unanchored your ship from the safety of the harbour. After all ships are meant to sail in the ocean!

- Observe the thoughts that come to your mind when you are idle, and busy.
- Pen down (or type/record) your thoughts as they come, without editing them, for a stipulated amount of time each day, even if it is for 5 minutes.
- After a week, or month, read to see what topics, what relations, what worries and opportunities are you constantly thinking about and what patterns emerge?
- Are they Appreciative? Angry? Other?
- Do you wish to reframe?
    o   If yes, ask yourself what is the gift you see in any situation or relation, good or bad?
    o   What has the presence of that situation or relation taught you?
    o   How far have you come and become who you are because of that?

o   What are you grateful about?
o   What is your choice now?

PS: It is helpful to stick 'What are you thinking?' or 'Observe your thoughts' in places that you frequently visit to help remind you to notice your thinking.

Binding or Bonding? ~

~ Letters to my grandchildren ~

My dear little ones, out of the many words you will learn starting with the alphabet 'B', I have a few fundamental ones to share. In addition to 'Bat' or 'Ball', words that helped me to understand the world, the outer world, I was curious to gain access to the mysterious inner world that exists within us. The secret to peace, happiness and fulfillment lies in there. Our inner world determines how we respond to the outer world - people, places and perspectives. Practicing the essence of the few fundamental words below has been life-giving, nourishing and key to expanding possibilities for me.

As you grow each day into beautiful beings, I invite you to experiment, play and discover the essence of these words in your life. As you master the game, you will get clues to master your life and create your own future that is meaningful, day-by-day. The key is to choose wisely and practice consciously. Remember, whatever you practice; consciously, sub-consciously, or unconsciously, right or wrong, it grows stronger. So, what do you choose?

B for 'Breath', the life source

- What values are the essentials in your life that no one can take away from you like the breath of life?
- What do you do to honour your own values and that of others, even if they are conflicting?

B for 'Beginnings'

- What do you discover about yourself of your readiness to explore beyond your comfort zone in thoughts, words and actions?

B for 'Being' and 'Becoming'

- What are your states of 'being' that enables you to become who you wish to be? What are other states of 'being' that is not helpful?

- What do you choose to 'become' as a person irrespective of how life and other people turn out to be?

Other words, also starting with 'B', also served me but only for short-term. Practice of the essence of these words fed my ego and exhausted me in the long-term as I found them to be life-depleting;

B for 'Boredom', 'Belittling others' and 'Beaten down'.

Practice of *Satsang* with Family – A Story

Binding or Bonding? ~

Aek baar (remember, it means once upon a time), there was a beautiful, brave, young Hungarian girl, who grew up in a town called Hatvan, few kms from Budapest. You already know her as your Hungarian grandmother, (& my dear friend, Bogi). We met in Singapore as AIESEC interns and became thick friends after a while, sharing stories day after day as flat mates over steaming hot cups of tea, about growing up in our respective families in different cultures, in different countries and continents.

On the exterior, our realities could not have been more different. She grew up with her mother. Her father had left their family when she was a little child. That was her first painful memory. She did not talk to him for a long while, only much later in life. Her circumstances taught her to be independent at a very young age, going to the market alone at the age of five to buy the needful. She learnt to take care of herself and her mother. She learnt to be disciplined sticking to her strict routine of weekly 30 hours of aerobics and gymnasium (her own anchoring moments in every-day life).

This was a truly amazing story for me; a complete nerd in my childhood, whose only strict routine was to complete her home work for school and study, possibly 30 hours too in a week! I was not allowed to go anywhere beyond school and 3 kms of my home alone. I grew up in the safe cocoon with my grandparents primarily. My only work out was verbal; the conversations and story sessions with *nanima, nanaji,* my parents, aunts, cousins and relatives. Bogi's story sessions were only and mostly with the television.

The more we listened to each other, the more we appreciated the pieces in the story – of the other. The grass always looked greener on the other side.

Scratch the exterior away; we realized we had many similarities in our dreams, hopes and aspirations even though we came from different parts of the world. We were both quite resolute too to fulfill our dreams and create the lives we had imagined for ourselves. One underpinning common childhood dream that had come true for both of us was to go overseas, to explore the world, other cultures, other ways of life. I did not know about Hungary in my childhood, just as she did not know about India, in her childhood. Yet, little surprise that we did not deter even minutely to travel afar, to each other's countries, when the opportunity arose.

Bogi visited India way before I visited Hungary. Independent as she was, she began to carve out her travel plans much earlier than I did. Of the many places she saw on National Geographic, she was attracted to India, and later as we will know in this story, also to a special Indian.

Speaking of decision-making, she relied on her imagination and all what her experience had taught her. Her mother too relied on her daughter for decision - making. Her mother herself had not traveled far and wide and did not have the experience that her daughter's imagination warranted. She readily accepted Bogi's decision to travel to India for the first time in life. However, Bogi felt caught on the cross-roads of a decision, especially when her grandmother fell ill after all the plans were made. Bogi spoke about her dilemma – to go or not to go. She shared that she did not wish to be a selfish person and wondered what was right. Her grandmother looked her in the eye and said, 'You owe it to yourself to live your life to the fullest. You do not owe your life to me. Choose such that you do not regret your decisions later on in life.' She felt assured in her inner world, felt secure of her family bonds and decided to make the trip of her dreams. She soon set forth for India.

Speaking of my decision-making for my life, it seemed to rely on everyone else's imagination but my own! I could not help but laugh when I would tell my story to Bogi that back in India, when I had desired to apply for my university beyond Darjeeling, in Delhi, I had some thousands of rounds of conversations. The conversations continued with my grandparents and my parents, my parents with other parents, relatives, teachers and family members. There were many opinions, advises, perspectives and even decisions cast for me. My aunts who had brought me up understood me and lovingly supported me. Some extended family members and relatives were not so happy. Some even decided for my parents that I SHOULD NOT go. Some called me childish and others chided me for my crazy dreams. It was a bad idea and an impediment for my marriage.

I could put the family name at risk. How about trusting me and getting to know me than making judgments from afar, I would sullenly think. How could I explain to them that not taking a risk in life was the biggest risk? I would desperately think.

I was deeply grateful for the few family members and my schoolteachers who saw the potential in me, as they had seen me work astutely towards getting the marks that would prove my worth when I approached universities. My family was proud of me after seeing my name as the topper on the school board that gave them confidence to take the risk for me. Looking back, I shared with Bogi the extreme emphasis on marks and competition in the education system that I came from. I was not the best, but I had worked really hard and prayed even harder! She was more intrigued by the competition in the family system.

Finally, after what seemed like the Mahabharata of my age and time, my parents decided in my favour. It was a first to send a young girl beyond Darjeeling. It was a first to send a young girl to big, bad Delhi, to pursue higher education in our family history. I gulped. I realized it was not easy for my parents. In this war, my parents were my shields. They encouraged me to check out Kolkata (Calcutta) universities first, as it was closer to home. I agreed, albeit reluctantly. Clear on the action route, my parents and younger brother soon set forth for Kolkata, to check out the colleges and hostels – interestingly, without me! I found that strange, mildly speaking! Bogi could not stop laughing!!!

On a serious note, I had one additional choice to be considered for my inner peace. Like Bogi, I felt guilty about leaving my grandmother. What would happen to *nanima* if I left her? Perhaps it would not be so bad after all to study in the local university of my small town, a small voice in my head nagged at me. Yet, something deep in me knew that I had to go. The pros and cons of my decision played a ferocious game of table-tennis in my head. I took a deep breath, decided to accept the ball in my court and initiated this difficult conversation with *nanima*. Knowing me far too well by then, she knew that my decision was made, even if I was not completely sure of myself. She simply said, "Girls are expected to leave home after they are grown up. I will just think that you are married." I smiled at the thought of being married to my dreams – quite a unique idea!

Emboldened and more at peace, after Kolkata, I requested my parents to check out Delhi too. I was thrilled when my parents took me along this time. We all decided for Lady Shri Ram College for Women. Bogi has always teased me about going to an all-girls' university but this is natural for many in India. Due to the admission procedures, my parents agreed to stay for more than a month in New Delhi. Dad missed his work in the mean time. My brother missed his school. My mother even met with an accident but stayed strong and we stayed put. My aunts took care of my grandparents while we were away. It was my most powerful lesson about strong family bonds and collaboration, rising above any competition. It was a triumph for all when I got admissions, and also got the much sought after hostel seat too. Everyone was at peace. I peacefully accepted the piece of advice from my father that independence is truly to be in-dependence, feeling connected with family, in all its stages of evolving and becoming. Incredible!

Meanwhile, Incredible India, as is known widely in tourist circles, was an eye-opener for Bogi, in her own words. She realized that all that she had seen on television and documentaries gave her a biased picture. Coming from the developed Western world, she was gladly surprised to see that the metropolitan cities like New Delhi were well-developed and the standards of living were high. People were affluent, fluent in English – infact, far better than the levels conversed in, back in Hungary. There was poverty as well, but what surprised her much was to see what she called, 'extreme positivity'. She saw it in the eyes of many people from diverse backgrounds, who would rush to take photographs with her wherever she went. She noticed how happy people were even if they were poor. They had wide smiles and were very hospitable. She laughed that she has no idea on how many Indian family albums she would find herself with smiling strangers. She fell in love with India and was determined to return.

As fate would have it, soon enough, back in Hungary, she fell in love with an Indian prince charming, who was staying with her and her mother in Hungary, completing his internship. She stood her ground in the face of any mockery for her "brown boyfriend" who was referred to as 'gypsy', 'exotic' etc. She was serious about their relationship. They decided to be in Asia. She was ready to leave Europe, a first in her family history, secure that her mother was fine with her decision. He did not want to return to India yet, so he found a job

21

in China. She came for an internship to Singapore. Strong on a long-distance relationship, they finally had a precious chance to visit India together for his cousin's wedding. He wanted her to meet his family. She was thrilled, waiting in anticipation to visit India, the land she had fallen in love with, with the love of her life.

His parents hosted her very well. She thoroughly enjoyed immersing in the rich Indian culture that pans out widely in a wedding, meeting his friends and cousins, getting to know about his life intimately. She returned to Singapore full of precious stories about her 'in-laws-to-be'. She definitely wanted an Indian wedding. She was ready to accept the new family, new culture, new life.

It came nothing short of a heart-wrenching shock for her, and for us, when she got to know that his family had not approved of her as his wife-to-be. They desired for him to marry an Indian girl. But she thought that they had really liked her. She did not understand why.

She turned to her immediate family – one that she was not born into but had chosen and created strong bonds with – family of friends from across the globe in Singapore. She asked us incessantly of her blind spots – Did she do anything wrong? How might she make it all right? How might she reach out to his family? She did not know 'why' and 'How to change things?'

She spoke to her mother, breaking the news to her, of the second-most significant heart-break after her father. Her mother stood by her, calling her everyday and listening to her, being there for her, but could not answer, the 'why'. We all realized how much our loved ones offer support, be it from afar, when life knocks you down.

She finally turned to him to seek answers. He explained that it was not about her. His family had grudgingly accepted all those years when he told them that he had a Hungarian girlfriend. However, they had secretly hoped that it was only a phase that would end naturally. They were rather alarmed when he brought her home and persisted to continue into marriage. They could not accept that. They would not accept that. On the other hand, he could not think of standing up against his family. Their bonds were too strong. He concluded, "I cannot start a new beginning of my life without my family's consent. I owe it to my family". This was a new concept for her as she was taught that she owes nothing to her family but only to the future she creates for herself, through her choices and commitment. She was committed to him. Not only that, it was a new concept for her that they could accept her as his girlfriend for years, but not as his wife. She had not felt anything amiss while she was with them. She did not understand, even more.

Neither did us, her global family. It was akin to two different worldviews that were meeting for the first time. I remember once I was late and Bogi had to wait for me. She had explained how that was offensive to her for it meant that I did not value her time. Where she was coming from, it was considered really rude to not be punctual. I was taken aback as I had no intention to offend her or to be rude. I found her way of thinking very rigid. I told her so that if I did not feel relaxed and authentic, it would scare me the next time we meet on a Sunday where I would be stressed to keep time on the dot as if I were going for a professional meeting. She found my way of thinking very non-committal especially when I berated her to carry a book to keep her engaged if I am late in the future. Over time, we both learnt to empathise with each other. Underneath the thoughts, our friendship mattered and we found a middle way. She carried a book. I improved on my punctuality and it was a high when on some occasions, I made it before her! We were willing to learn each other's ways and change our mindsets or worldviews because it mattered to the other person.

Looking at different mindsets, especially those regarding marriage and family bonds in different cultures, or even between families from the same culture, we wondered when does it become binding and constricting?

My family had loved me and hence made sure that they were with me every step of the way to ensure that I get my admissions in my dream college. Her family had loved her and hence made sure that they get out of the way and let her pursue her dream of traveling and make the most of opportunities. His family had loved him and hence had predicted that he would be happier if he married an Indian girl just like everyone else in his family tree had done so. They advocated for an arranged marriage, another mindset that was a complete novelty for Bogi. He had loved his family and chose their decision over his. He still loved her too but did not know how to convince his family.

Is 'The individual versus the collective' so ingrained in us, in our decisions and behaviours in everyday life that we are blind to it? What is the truth that sets one free?

Once eleven friends from seven countries from Canada to China were sitting in Malaysia and chitchatting. For one friend from Canada, it made perfect sense to stop working and travel the world for few years, explore the world and discover oneself. This way, one could focus on work and family later. For another friend from China, it was crazy to 'waste time' after their parents had spent a lifetime enabling them to get the education they had. It was considered lavish to take out time and money to spend on traveling. Both perspectives had a common in them. The respective ways of life was chosen for the sake of making the family unit stronger and healthier.

We were about to generalize that thought and behaviour for Canadians and Chinese when the more we listened to different people, the more we realized how much it all depended upon individuals and their choices, in spite of the backgrounds they came from. The conversations steered towards love, relationships, life and marriage. As we listened to all, it became clear that sometimes the distinctions from even the same country and culture are not as clear. A rainbow of choices appears. Closer to my home country, I have heard of some Indians speak of acceding to arranged-marriages simply so if anything goes wrong, they do not have to take responsibility and can blame their parents! Some say this in a light spirit. Some mean it seriously. Some agree to arranged-marriages to avoid missing on the fortune one might inherit, either through one's parents or through dowry. Some agree to arranged-marriages because they have to, helplessly. Some agree to arranged-marriages hopefully, willingly and fall in love after just as they had known they would. It is all very individualistic too and depends on 'who' one is interacting with. In relationship the 'who' of both individuals matter.

Every individual has her/his own truth known to her/him. It is a different story if one wishes to share the same with family or friends, or not.

Guess learning about bonds and love is a life - long journey of being and becoming both for individuals and families involved. Sometimes parents are the teachers and some other times, children are the teachers. It is about authentic communication of one's choices and wishes, so that everyone can make informed decisions and reduce pain in old and new relationships. Sometimes the choices fit the norm. Sometimes they do not. Sometimes, it is in the grey arena. Tongue-in-cheek, we drew a communication model where a lady should not only look out for if the man loves her, but also if the man would have the courage to share so of his love with his parents and convince his family. In addition, the lady needs to know if the man's family would accept their son's choice. What does that depend on? Usually, that respect has to be earned by young men and women by making other credible choices that the family is proud of. We also spoke if we could trust someone who leaves his family to be with the woman he loves?

Some of the Indian men in the group assured that it is not that bad when knowing oneself, one's own values and communicating them authentically from the start to the family, helps the family to accept that their child is different. Even if the family does not accept, the child is at peace, knowing that he/she has communicated well.

It is quite easy for many conscious men and women in love. Some love marriages end up as arranged marriages when the families agree. Closer to home, I cited the example of my tenacious cousin – Rachna Dalmia and her then sensitive, partnering boyfriend, Sumit Kumar. They are no longer boyfriend and girlfriend, I had shared. Though both are Indians, they come from different cultures and ethnicities. They were together for years helping each other grow, enabling each other's education and career despite the odds. They waited patiently and engaged their respective families for their consent to get married, especially my aunt, who was not willing to agree. I had seen Rachna and Sumit meet all obstacles head strong, or maybe it was heart strong, through months and years that finally dissolved all objections. Therefore, today, they are no longer boyfriend and girlfriend only but also husband and wife. They are married and the happy parents of my beautiful niece, Bhavya.

As Bogi's family in Singapore, and her close friends, we were really surprised when he returned to woo her after a year. He had regretted his decision and wanted to be with her. It had dawned upon him how much he had learnt, growing up in his internship, hosted by her and her mother in Hungary and how happy he had been with her. He admitted that he loved her for his total acceptance of him and that he could share everything with her, when he could not do so even with his parents. Bogi loved him and readily got back together despite our discomfort. She wanted us to be happy for them. It all seemed to work well. It all seemed like a Bollywood movie. We teased them about a big, colourful, Indian wedding. It seemed like a new beginning.

New beginnings can however lead the way back to the old endings, if new consciousness and new actions is not part of the journey.

Although he had expressed his feelings eloquently to Bogi, he could not do so with his family, again. Only after she had agreed, did he bravely go back to talk to his family. His family had already laid out their reasons and perspectives. They did not consent. Finally, he turned to Bogi and said, "I do not want but I have to break up again". He had decided, again, for both of them, leaving her with little choice.

Breathe in! Breathe out! Life continues as long as one breathes!

Staying in Singapore stoically, Bogi finally concluded one evening, steering away from right and wrong perspective that she had always wanted to understand a different culture and what it meant to have family bonds. This was her first hand experience where she did get the opportunity to understand a different culture and a different kind of family bond! The universe decides to give what you want in unexpected colours some times. Like she did not get what she imagined but felt blessed for her new-found family in a foreign land; friends, who had stood by her side witnessing the thick and the thin. We all admitted we did not know and hence could not appreciate the depths of the struggles he might have undergone too, knowing only one side of the story, Bogi's side. We just hoped for each one of us to find our respective life partners, and strengthen our families and ourselves for our future and our future generations.

We learnt the invaluable lesson to know firstly, what one wants out of a relationship and to articulate that with courage and compassion. Secondly, it is ok to question even in a budding new romance, where that might be going and if all goes well, would the family of the partner be accepting? What would the partner's stand be if the family disagrees? Gauging the answers from there, listening to the heard and the unheard, one can choose the paths ahead or atleast be aware even if one is going with the flow.

Some people live with the choices their family makes for them.

Some families live with the choices their family member makes for the self.

Some people know the art of involving their families and vice versa.

Some families have safe structures that allow the members of the family to reveal their truths and get to know each other truly.

Ultimately, some adapt to their futures because they have to while some create their futures because they want to. Who are you and how do you relate to your family (the one you are born into and/or the one you create consciously in this life time)? What blind spots have you learnt from?

One cannot underestimate how worthwhile it is to honestly invest in the family bonds before sailing out together on a ship without a common destination. Then it is worthwhile to test those bonds, when the waters get rough. Do they survive? In any case, what are your choices?

I hope and pray for you that you feel strengthened by bonds of love in your inner world and in your relationships in life. I trust you to practice the art of engaging your heart and that of others towards a future that is truly freeing.

Best wishes for becoming the person of your dreams,

Yours Grandma

PS: So, my lovely grandchildren, what are your stories of valuing hard work and heart work, as your *Practice of Satsang*, in your times?

"Live fully, love truly and look for opportunities for spiritual growth"

-Bogi Inkret (2014)
(Happiness Coach, Consulting Hypnotist
and Munay-ki Master, the ancient initiation of the Incas)

Now, it is time for Practice.
You may create your own or experiment with one I suggest below.

Practice
(B)

To create strong bonds of understanding and love. Strong bonds built on healthy foundations enables further empathy, deeper listening and caring for each other in both good and bad times.

- Take out time to engage one who matters, irrespective of your perception of the person as easy-going or difficult/impossible.

- Disclosure –
  o Share your important dream with the individual.
  o Also share the related fears and hopes.
  o Share more about who you are as a person and why is the dream important for you. Share about the context, your values and other meaningful things.
  o If need be, request for help from the person, irrespective of whether the other can or chooses to help or not.
  o Notice your state of being throughout.

- Dialogue –
  o Ask the same individual about her/his dream
  o Tune up your listening ears. Listen as if you are to quote her/him.
  o See what they see. See as if you are she/he.

- o   Offer what help you can and follow-up on it, without any expectations.
- o   Notice the state of becoming of this relationship.

PS: It is helpful to breathe deeply when you feel nervous, afraid, angry, excited etc to attain equanimity.

Complicated Challenges, Courageous Choices ~

~ Letters to my grandchildren ~

My dear little ones, out of the many words you will learn starting with the alphabet 'C', I have a few fundamental ones to share. In addition to 'Cat' or 'Chair', words that helped me to understand the world, the outer world, I was curious to gain access to the mysterious inner world that exists within us. The secret to peace, happiness and fulfillment lies in there. Our inner world determines how we respond to the outer world - people, places and perspectives. Practicing the essence of the few fundamental words below has been life-giving, nourishing and key to expanding possibilities for me.

As you grow each day into beautiful beings, I invite you to experiment, play and discover the essence of these words in your life. As you master the game, you will get clues to master your life and create your own future that is meaningful, day-by-day. The key is to choose wisely and practice consciously. Remember, whatever you practice; consciously, sub-consciously, or unconsciously, right or wrong, it grows stronger. So, what do you choose?

C for 'Compassion'

- What blessings do you see in your life as you see compassion by family, friends, strangers expressed towards you and others?
- What do you practice to develop compassion for yourself and others in all situations?

C for 'Courage'

- Who is your role model for courage?
- When are moments in your life when you have expressed courage and what called for it?

C for 'Choice' and 'Commitment' to Desired Change

- What do you commit to, even as life is evolving?

- What choices do you make to stay true to yourself in practice?

Other words, also starting with 'C', also served me but only for short-term. Practice of the essence of these words fed my ego and exhausted me in the long-term as I found them to be life-depleting;

C for 'Cynicism', 'Compromise' and 'Criticizing' (Different from 'Critique' which is healthy).

Practice of *Satsang* with Family – A Story

Complicated Challenges, Courageous Choices ~

This is the story of a young Indian boy from a business, conventional family, who mustered his courage to go up to his father and state that he wanted to study Law. Now, this was in the 1970s where the general trend was for the boys to get into the family business at a young age.

That was supposed to be the right way. Simple.

However, one of his older brothers was a gold medalist and had pursued his education in Engineering. Yet, post education, his brother had to join the family business too. Hence, the father asked the young boy, "What is the point of investing in your studies?" The young boy determinedly answered, "I will help out in the family business and balance it by practising my law practice too." If his father agreed, he would be the first boy in the family who would have a different line of trade.

The young boy grew up to be a young man, a young Advocate by profession, a businessman by virtue of keeping his promise, a caring son, a fierce and fun uncle to his nephews and nieces and all-in-all, a good man. All of these were signals enough that he was ready for marriage.

His father called him one day and showed him photographs of a girl whom he thought would be good for his son. The young man heard that she was a bright, convent educated girl, fluent in English, a smart lady and the eldest daughter of a family with only sisters. No brother! Usually that would be an impediment in an arranged marriage setting for many girls, again re-emphasizing the importance of a boy in those times. But his father was ok with that. They would get a good dowry. The girl's father was a renowned businessman. The family was respectable. They came from a bigger town. These were some of the considerations for arranged marriages. These were hardly the considerations for the young man. He wandered wondering if he would make a good husband and if he were ready. If the others said that he was ready, he guessed he was!

That was supposed to be the right way. Simple. He agreed to marry the girl shown in the photograph.

The young man met the girl for the first time on their Engagement ceremony. (Imagine that!) They got to know each other thereafter through posting hand-written letters. (When is the last time you wrote a letter, not a mail or a SMS, but a hand-written letter to somebody? Wonder if hand-written letters are prevalent in your times! I ask the same questions to myself and find myself lost for an answer!) Finally, the wedding day arrived. It was a grand wedding.

He was curious about his wife. She was smart, courteous and carried herself with dignity, akin to an uptown girl. His friends mercilessly teased him that finally, he would have to brush up his English. He smiled nervously knowing that so far he had been writing his letters in Hindi. He wondered if he had time in his hectic schedule to take up English classes. He wanted to be a husband his wife would be proud of.

With the passage of time, he completely fell in love with his wife. That was supposed to be the right way – arranged marriage first, love later. Simple. Yet, irrespective of what was right or wrong, he really admired her for her grit and determination. She had taken great pains to adjust to his large joint family.

His wife had learnt to navigate from cooking for a six-person family to cook for about a twenty-six person's family. In the smaller town, akin to a village where they were living then, they almost never had any electricity. Initially, it might have been romantic to have a candle-lit dinner but when that becomes the norm, the romance evaporates. She would have to do all the kitchen work in the darkness. So did everyone else. The difference was that she was very afraid of the dark. It became a family joke to listen to her occasional shrieks every time she would encounter cockroaches or other creepy-crawly creatures. She adapted and adjusted and did her best. He was proud of her.

He saw much potential in her and encouraged her to take up the job of a teacher in the only English school in their small town-village. He was sure her contribution would be relevant. She liked the idea, however was dubious of the prospect. She would be the first lady in the family to work if that happened. It would not be that simple.

He went to seek permission from his father. His father was supportive, though his mother was not too happy with the prospect. She dismissively said that if her daughter-in-law wanted to teach, she could do so as long as the housework was not compromised. That was a tall order to balance in that big joint family; the cooking chores, the washing of dishes, the cleaning, the lack of facilities and amenities like electricity and even water (many a time, they had to pull water up from the well), the management of the household with many other women!

It was not as simple as it looked. His wife declined the role of a teacher in order to be a worthy housewife. The role of a housewife has been undermined for far too long. It was not a battle worth fighting for.

He would often speak of the pros and cons of a joint family with his wife. She had grown up in a cozy nuclear family environment. Married in a large family, it was a culture shock for her. The huge family gatherings, celebrations, rituals, squabbles were all quite new for her. She had never experienced kitchen politics in her small family before the wedding. She had been taught the value of collaboration and was taken aback by competition in the big family system.

Life goes on. Life is much about learning and unlearning. While at it, the couple had their first child, and then the second. The circle of life continued.

One year, his aging father-in-law, one of the best businessmen of the bigger town, was struck with some ill luck, where the business collapsed. He heard his relatives say that that was why it was important to be part of the joint family or have sons. One might say that a business collapse is easier to be absorbed by a big, joint family than that run by a single person. It is debatable though because the response to crisis depends not so much on the size of the family, rather the security of family ties and the willingness to support each other to overcome any crisis. In a debate, one wins and the other loses. In life, one lives and learns, the best one can.

His wife was fearful for her parents' health and well-being. As the eldest child in the family, she felt responsible and attached to her family and wanted to offer support. As a woman, married, in a different town, she had no idea about what or how. She just wished she could do more as a daughter than was allowed.

It was complicated.

He wanted his wife to be happy and at peace. As the eldest son-in-law, he felt empathetic. As a man, married, in a different town, with some awareness of the changing times and its impact on businesses in the bigger town, he knew that times were still not modern enough for him to step up to help because he was the son-in-law, and not the son. Personally, it made no difference to him as he perceived relationships that mattered as One big joint family after all.

It was complex.

However, his conscience would not settle down for the excuse of doing nothing just because he was a son-in-law. Keen to address than simply ignore the challenge, he began a dialogue with his wife exploring various options. One evening, over a cup of *chai*, they were in deep thoughts. Would it be insane if she moved to the bigger town and stayed with her parents, took care of them, who would after all only grow weaker as old age caught up? The distance between the towns was only a few hours and he could easily travel to and fro to spend time with her in the weekends. Perhaps over time, if he found reasonable resources and opportunities, he might even think of re-locating.

It was a bold step. It was risky. But it was compelling. It was another first, with no such precedent in the family or community. It was just plain wrong, for some.

The right way for a woman is to look after her in-laws and not her parents after marriage. The right way for a man is to think of his family and his parents and not necessarily, his in-laws after marriage. However, those right ways that are defined by culture do not serve some individuals and collectives. In the absence of any other right ways, one might react and rebel. The outcomes for that are not far-reaching as when thoughtful and conscious creative solutions are sought.

Sometimes in the face of complexity, the correct creative answers come from within, than without. The young man and his wife both shared similar values of balancing their resources for the family. They hoped that their combined resources would support their ailing parents, and be invaluable lessons of values for their children. It only seemed right to give the unique solution he had proposed a try. Unless one tries, one never knows. It seemed worthwhile to take the risk than not to care at all. It required courage to commit to the choice. It required double courage to share it with the other family members and stand one's ground. It required triple doses of courage to take the risk, without knowing the outcome and doing the best one can, given the circumstances. It was their truth. They rose to it.

If we do not challenge cultural norms according to new circumstances that arise, who will? If we do not care, can we live happily with that consciousness?

Every generation has had some people who adapt, some who challenge, some who compromise, some who care more for change, some who create and some who criticize. The couple faced all varying kinds of reactions from different generations to the change they proposed to act upon. Together, the couple enfolded one member after another, into their decision and began to step towards the desired changes.

This courageous couple, my grandchildren, is your great grandparents and my parents. They have been the pioneers of conscientious change in our family tree that has enabled the growth of consciousness in relationships.

I saw all of it unfold like a movie in front of me. I was ecstatic when I heard that my mother and my younger brother were moving to my town and coming to stay with us and that dad would visit us every now and then, unlike before! Sure, the fact that I was staying at my grandparent's place since very young must have enabled their decision in some ways, thickening the plot. The climax of that part of the movie series was when the towns, the families, the friends were all astounded and my aunts, married by then, were happy and relieved that my parents had chosen courageously to create a different route to nurture our family tree. I was happy that as a family we were reaping the harvest of seeds that were sown ages ago.

It was simple after all.

Truth be told, it was simple only once I allowed it. Initially, I was quite mad and did not quite want mother to move in with us. It was time of my life when

I learnt about the comfort zone, and how closed that can make a person. I remember the early storm days, when I would fight with my mother, not understanding a thing, and refusing to reflect. After a week of cold war, when I had not spoken to her, she came up to me one day and asked for a conversation. She opened up trustingly and shared some personal stories of her childhood days. It explained why she was protective of me and wanted to teach me things that every mother wants her child to learn. A little voice in my head that I had been ignoring for a while finally whispered out aloud, "You have missed your mother throughout. Now that she is here, stop the drama and connect."

Living with the two generations, my parents and grandparents were the golden years of my life. I got a chance to grow with my mother, for the first time. I regressed to be a child and unabashedly gave a hard time to my younger brother and your grandparent–uncle, Sheshank, the smarter one of the two. Though we were siblings, we had never had the chance to grow up together, so we started afresh-fight, fight, fight till we get it right! What fun to be blessed with a sibling!

Evolving together as a family, we swam in the tides of change with people who mattered.

My father's wish, ultimately, did come true – my mother did become a teacher. She taught her family, leading by example, life-lessons about compassion, courage, choice and commitment. She taught diverse subjects role-modeling as a daughter, as a mother, as a wife, as the eldest sister. My choice to do a job and journey from Siliguri to Singapore would not have materialized had it not been for mother making the attempt to understand me, and more importantly, for standing up for me. She takes much flak from family and relatives for years. As a faithful gardener, she just pulls the weeds of hesitation, jealousy, anger away, over and over again.

Yet, some tenacious ones of doubt resurface every now and then, when she questions her life choices. She wonders if she made the wrong choices, putting her husband and children in difficult situations. Little does she realize that we are in awe of her commitment despite the difficulties she faced courageously. I see her as a true practitioner of *satsang*, sharing herself wholly to help uplift energies around her, be it for her parents, children, husband or other. She is my *guru* who taught me to celebrate the truth of who you are. She taught me to build a relation with the self, as much as one builds it with another. She listens to all my thoughts coming from ego and the heart about my relationships, my work, my dreams and my life and helps me choose the truth and choices that are of higher frequency and service to myself and others, over and over again. Of course there are often times when I do not listen to her. She still accepts my choices and is there for me in my downs, as much as in my ups.

Open communication with parents is possible.

When a friend asked me about the one thing I would change in my relationship with my children that I miss from my relationship with my parents, I shuddered. I hope I can be courageously loving enough to give to my children what my parents gave to me. It is easier to say not to be judgmental or attached to the point of stifling than to practice suspending judgments and truly balance attachment and detachment.

I saw a little girl in mother and also a wise old woman, much older than her current age. Perhaps all of have that child within us and the wise, old soul too and celebrating all the shades is the way to be.

Mother took up the responsibilities of *nanima,* becoming a mother-like-figure to her younger sisters. She always reminds me to be responsible too as I am the elder sibling, to which I opportunistically respond that since I was brought up by *nanima,* I am her younger sibling!

Life's flow is mysterious and balanced. Despite my smart-aleck responses, I admired mother when she faithfully attended to take care of her youngest sister, Babita, who was in the winter of her life when her marriage and mental peace had been like a storm in the sea. We all witnessed mother flow and help flow and ensure that no boat capsizes. One day, when I tried to tell her that I admire her, mother quietly shrugged and reminded me that I should also admire Babita *masi* (my aunt), whose strengths then were hidden under the 'snow'. In the summer of her life, Babita had helped me step confidently into the spring of my childhood. It is nothing but the circle of life!

It was then that I learnt about the internal seasons of life, which sometimes may be different from the external seasons. I also learnt to believe that seasons change.

In the ocean of learning in our family, little did my father know that in enabling and supporting his wife and her family, he turned out to be a visionary Principal; a unique one, different from men of his age and time in the patriarchal reality. He embodied teamwork with his wife and many others who rose to the occasion. One of his deepest strengths was his own attitude and ability to learn in varying circumstances and to engage the very best of people. Rising to his own personal best, he strengthened the 'joint' family roots looking both after his own father in his old age especially when he was sick and supporting his father-in-law too. He chose to be a son, irrespective of the son-in-law tag. He has lived up to what I have read about Confucius' filial piety, teaching his children by example. I believe he listened more to the call of his soul than to the call of society.

I see my parents creating a family school of life that would grow stronger for and with each future generation. I have been a student and teacher in this.

I hope and pray for you that you face your challenges in compelling ways too that bring peace in your inner world and in your relationships. I trust you to practice to commit to what you believe in.

Crazily trusting you,

Grandma

PS: So, my lovely grandchildren, what are your stories of converting criticism from the fences to caring deeply about a cause, as your *Practice of Satsang*, in your times?

"Live a full life by nourishing lives of those you can. Always be humble and happy."

Shashi Dalmia (2013)
(*Mother*, Homemaker & Life maker)

"Be rich in inner happiness and peace by working and doing what is right for you. Remember to serve, be grateful and celebrate the blessings that you receive too."

-Ashok Dalmia (2013)
-(*Father*, Super Hero & Advocate)

Now, it is time for Practice.
You may create your own or experiment with one I suggest below.

Practice
(C)

To honour the ones who matter whom you admire, or wish to admire, for having made courageous choices in the face of challenges.

* Think of a person/s you admire, or wish to admire, as your role model.
* Imagine a movie casting them as the protagonist/s.
    o What message would you wish to convey to the audience?
    o How does your role model inspire you in your life?
    o What is the strength that you see (never mind the weaknesses)?
* You can interview your role model to get the depth of the story. 'Hire' the children in the family to interview the elders because there is something about the way the elders respond to children. Children, in return, genuinely wish to listen to the story and naturally sandwich their own curious questions in between.

- Play with storytelling, directing and promoting this movie and script. You may be a scriptwriter, cartoonist, short video maker, a storyteller or an artist.
- The key is to share this with your role model/s, and others.
- What can you do to contribute to the story further or continue the legacy?

PS: It is helpful to also honour yourself and feel inspired for your moments of courage when you have stayed true to your commitment that matters.

Dreams, Dance and Drum rolls ~

~ Letters to my grandchildren ~

My dear little ones, out of the many words you will learn starting with the alphabet 'D', I have a few fundamental ones to share. In addition to 'Dog' or 'Door', words that helped me to understand the world, the outer world, I was curious to gain access to the mysterious inner world that exists within us. The secret to peace, happiness and fulfillment lies in there. Our inner world determines how we respond to the outer world - people, places and perspectives. Practicing the essence of the few fundamental words below has been life-giving, nourishing and key to expanding possibilities for me.

As you grow each day into beautiful beings, I invite you to experiment, play and discover the essence of these words in your life. As you master the game, you will get clues to master your life and create your own future that is meaningful, day-by-day. The key is to choose wisely and practice consciously. Remember, whatever you practice; consciously, sub-consciously, or unconsciously, right or wrong, it grows stronger. So, what do you choose?

D for 'Dreams'

- What blessings do you see in your life as you see your dreams come true or the struggles they bring to you so you may learn and evolve?
- What do you practice to help others develop their dreams?

D for 'Dialogue' and 'Deep Listening'

- Think of a time when you felt you were alive with others in conversations that truly mattered to all of you. What made it special?
- Whom do you choose to listen to and focus on - the other person speaking or that familiar voice in your own head?

D for 'Designing'

- Who do you admire as a designer – of life?

- What do you wish to design or create in life that will benefit you, your generation and the next too?

Other words, also starting with 'D', also served me but only for short-term. Practice of the essence of these words fed my ego and exhausted me in the long-term as I found them to be life-depleting;

D for 'Defensive', 'Depressed' and 'Damaged'.

Practice of *Satsang* with Family – A Story

Dreams, Dance and Drum rolls ~

"I have a dream ..."

"I want to be a great parent"(or "grandparent", "brother", "sister", "aunt" ...)

"I want to be a child my parents can be proud of."

"I want to be loved for who I am. My family does not really understand me."

"My legacy is my family – I hope they love each other even when I am gone."

"I am bringing my children the way I was brought up – This way I hope to transfer family values, though my children say times have changed!"

"I wish my parents would not fight so much."

"I wish I could talk to my mother/father who left us when we were young."

"I hope one day I can talk to that family member and understand him/her."

"I want my wife to get along well with my mother."

"I want my husband to build relations with my family."

"I wish my parents were not divorced."

"I want to learn to forgive and be forgiven for my mistakes."

"I wish my family would get over the grief and move on."

"I dream of my family as loving, growing, nurturing, caring, and happy."

Myriads of such dreams and aspirations fill the space across time that our human species wish to fulfill. Family is often a primary unit that has an impact on individuals, right from when they are most vulnerable as children, in need of love, care and protection. The psyche of the family members, the history of the family tree, the bonds of connectedness, the roots of identity or lack of any or some of it has a huge impact. It is a perpetual dance from generation to generation irrespective of whether one gets stuck or one flows. The movement is inevitable. The consciousness of where one comes from, where one is, where one wishes to go helps.

Relationships that matter try and test us and can bring out the best and the worst in us.

Once upon a time, in every family, there was an Anybody who shared her/his dream. Then there was an Everybody who laughed at and ridiculed the idea. Somebody quietly supported and gave wings to the idea. Anybody can take the first step. When Anybody can do it, Everybody is convinced of the possibility of the dream.

Are you that Anybody, Somebody or Everybody with yourself, your family members and with others?

I asked many people, primarily my peers, just in conversation, as an informal survey, what would their messages be for themselves, their own generation, the older generation and finally, for their grandchildren, born and yet to be born, or for the future generations?

There was one essence for everybody I 'interviewed' irrespective of her or his age, gender, gender orientation, marital status, nationality, race, religion or culture. We all hope for a better future for ourselves, with our children and grandchildren, with our loved ones.

We all hope that the world will not end in our lifetime or the next. Many blame the older generations and the current ones for many familial, communal, local and global problems. Some are in awe of all that had been achieved in the face of obstacles till date and are gentler and grateful to the older generation, taking responsibility to make things better in our times. Others are a mix of appreciation, understanding, critical questioning and criticism. Yet, everyone still believes and wants to create a different reality, of doing things differently and effectively for a better world for multi-generations.

We all hope that both the world and the people in it will evolve to elevated education, consciousness and practices that will serve our children, grandchildren and us. We find meaning in life believing that our presence, values and lineage will be able to contribute further in the process of life.

We know that some realization of dreams will happen in our lifetime. We also know that some other realization of dreams and desired changes will go beyond our lifetime, and that we will meet our death before our dreams come true. Yet, they are compelling enough to attend to, to start acting upon now.

The answers are no different than those of the older generations when asked what they remember of theirs and their parents' and grandparents' dreams and times. Their parents and grandparents had faced trials and tribulations of their times. Many families across the globe have had a history of being affected by wars, uncertainty, economic stress, health concerns and various complexities. The families have passed through it all with hope for themselves and their future generations that are us, hoping for a continuity of all that they had nurtured in a lifetime. Some have lived to see their families survive and thrive. Others have passed away but their families remember them for their sheer strengths that helped them survive in tough times.

As one continues to understand the choices they have made, walking with them across and on the ragged mountain top with its high peaks and valleys, deeply listening to their reality of their times, one understands where they are coming from. Trek further and you will find that even underneath the most seemingly selfish design laid fear and anger and the need for self-protection of oneself and one's loved ones. If one ventures deeper into the wilderness to listen to the true base of the drumbeat, it is indeed a wish to make one's lifetime count. It is indeed to ensure that the next generation gets a better deal. Sure, some of their choices have endangered our very planet and the impact is far away from their intent. Yet, what choices is our generation making, currently, with our awareness, technology and practices?

Generation gap can be over-rated if there is no attempt made to connect, to listen, to learn from, to understand, to appreciate the story of the other. Sure, every generation differs from the preceding and the following ones. Yet, when you dig deeper to understand the inner worlds across generations, many similarities emerge despite the differences in the outer worlds. Irrespective of one's generation, one can only truly connect to the other when both make an attempt to co-create a safe space to converse and to share, to teach and to learn, both ways.

This is when many of my peers agree on how it is important to look after one's family surely, but also to understand how we are all inter-connected and hence to look after each other's families too. Some families are what we are born into. Some families are what we are married into. Some families are what we create, locally and globally, consciously with a different consciousness.

As one's understanding and love for people and planet expands, the dream of protecting people beyond one's own family, race, religion, nationality, and care for all species and life itself across time and space begins to take shape. Generation after generation have consciously or unconsciously wondered of a design that can give answers, atleast clues, to the questions of their times and to the questions future generations may have. Perhaps treating the globe as one big family might offer unique solutions what separating the globe and its resources and people could not offer.

Testing this out and reaching out, I have felt as a family member to even strangers in such conversations, in the sharing of dreams, related pains and challenges. I walked away from each of those conversations inspired, feeling more for the person and her/his family and the background the person came from. The idea of oneness vis-à-vis separateness, which was only in my cognitive domain for a long time, found new life and heartbeat as I tuned in to different rhythms of heartbeats with my own family members and with people across the planet.

Do you feel like an Anybody, Somebody, Everybody or Nobody as you relate to yourself and the human species with its perfect imperfections?

I have also heard, seen and felt innumerable times how in today's world with even digital and virtual connectivity, we can feel extremely lonely and disconnected. Many yearn for a sense of rootedness and belongingness even in their own families and communities.

Some may be living solitarily but most often, even when people live with their families; parents, spouses, children, siblings, they are in wanting and in search for connections in the outside world, in the virtual world, which is ok but not if they cannot connect with themselves and with their families first.

They cannot seem to connect because they never learnt to do so.

What they learnt did not serve in building strong connections. Some learnt to build harsh exteriors, safe boundaries and strong walls in the pretext of being strong. What they only learnt later was that that alienates one further and further away even from oneself and one's family. Some learnt that it is a taboo to cry, to express emotions and even judges the innate need to belong. What they only learnt later was that humans make all gender and other social constructs, and that they can be changed.

Are we losing the art of story-telling and conversing with each other in the pretext of busyness and business? Do we forget that these are ancient practices that allows for knowledge to be passed on from generation to generation?

Some people have ever decreasing conversations with their families. Some people have fewer opportunities to even meet their parents or grandparents or children. Work, studies, travels, situations and lack of time and energy all combine to the list of causes. How does one share one's dreams, fears, thoughts, and emotions for one's journey and destination with one's loved ones then? Some are learning new ways, from children and grandchildren to stay in touch across the virtual world. Younger generations are eagerly stepping up to be teachers/students.

Yet, with all this technology, we still need to learn to have deeper conversations, intimate conversations, honest and authentic conversations with our families.

The question often is who takes the first step towards stewarding the truth in conversations, in learning and creating that intentional safe space, especially in a family? Is it possible for any person of any age, gender and status to step up? Is it possible to go beyond the genre of complains and isolation to dance to the music of connectedness, healing and integration?

The answer is anyone, who cares enough for it, can take the first step. A common myth exists that elders have to initiate and take care. Elders anyway do the best with what they know at times. My Romanian friend, Iunia, shared with me the Celestine Prophecies that says that sometimes children choose their families so that they can teach/show a path that was thought to be impossible, as possible. Children are also teachers to their parents. That was wonderful to hear. It was freeing for me.

Amongst my peers, I have heard of transformational experiences from friends, who took the first bold step. They did not feel equipped to intervene necessarily. They just cared enough to observe, acknowledge and share their truth, which may be different from reality. They had to connect and listen to their family members' truths, which were also different from reality. Then what or who construes reality? If not tested, we each create our own reality based on assumptions and believe them for years, if not for generations!

A story that truly touched me was when one of my dearest friends became the catalyst in transforming relationships in her family. It made me believe. It made others believe. Amidst warm-hearted conversations, I do not recall a single friend who did not have a wish that some things would be different in their families. Some were struggling to connect with their parents, others with their siblings, and yet others with their spouses, children or in-laws! The question always was, who would bell the cat?

Authenticity in acknowledging the family truths and taking the first step to address is the key, I learnt from many of my brave friends who chose not to carry the family drama forward. Even if we are family, each one is on one's own spiritual journey. One cannot take on the work that the spiritual journey is required of your family member, irrespective of how much you love your partner, child or parent.

If we do take on the spiritual work of another, it just makes matters worse. When finally one can take no more, the expressions are not mindful and are a result of anger or fear. My dearest friend, from the West, was always mindful of the relationship between love and family. Observing her own family, she saw her mother dependent on the family and father wanting to be independent and suffering on that account that the family did not offer him that. As I listened, it sounded familiar. I thought of my *nanaji,* even father and the similarities between an Indian family and a family from another country!

Parental dynamics always impact the children. As children, we wondered how might we find love and freedom. My friend *knew* her purpose of life to bring healing to her family. She believes that through her own relationship and forming of a family, she can perhaps teach her parents that one can be independent in a family, and that's called interdependence.

Many of my peers today are afraid of commitment. One has to practice this in doses. My friend, committed to bring joy and peace in her family attempted to understand where her father was coming from, and also where her mother was coming from.

After a grand dinner and laughter on the occasion of her last few days at home, she took the bull with her hands and struck a conversation on values, behaviours and impact with her father. She prodded on to understand why did he have his values, why did he practice them in the face of tumultuous waters, and was he even aware of the wall he may have invariably created for his wife and his children? She shared how she felt, what she saw and what informed her that became 'her truth'. Responding to his daughter's openness, and questions, he began to unravel 'his truth' and explained where he came from and why.

Seeing the two tap their feet, it was not long before her mother and her brother joined the dance too, sharing 'their respective truths' slowly. Over the next few days, together, they began to co-create a rhythm, tuning in to each other's heartbeats.

My brave friend had taken the first step. She has always wondered on how she could do more to help them see, understand and communicate their needs with each other around love, freedom and independence. She chose healing and love over helplessness and a range of emotions that does not truly help.

She realized that 'her truth' all those years ago had comprised with all that she had seen, heard and felt. Yet, so many times, we are limited in what we see and hear, and hence, in how we feel. She was only seeing events and patterns then and making her own conclusions based on them. Her conclusions, in turn, made her see the same events. Deeply listening and having an ongoing dialogue with different members of her family gave wings to 'her truth'. After five years, 'her truth' comprises not only what she sees, hears and feels but also what she understands, simply by having spoken to her parents. She now sees events and patterns and also the threads of thinking of her family members and their values and purpose. Once we learn, evolve and grow, it is easier to let go of the past.

Another dear friend, from the East, spoke of the impending death of his sister, who had had cancer. But as a family, their natural reaction was to evade the real issue, get angry and build walls around themselves so as to not to feel. Swimming in our conversations, he went home and chose to build relationships with each family member, bringing them together and sharing their anger, grief, pain and joys.

It convinced me that family stories evolve, change and that anybody can step up to initiate a dance of trust with loved ones. I have had my own share of courageous conversations with different members of the family. Today, I feel at peace and purposeful when cousins ask me how to build their relations with their parents.

It is possible. It is a life-long learning.

Anybody can step up. Sometimes it is a child. Sometimes, it is an adult. Sometimes, it is the elderly. It can be Anybody who notices Somebody in a moment of vulnerability and reaches forward to ease the pain, even if Nobody acknowledges the pain.

I have had many 'Anybody' in my life at crucial junctions. I try to be one for others too. One of the turning points for me was when I was getting cold feet before flying off to another city for my studies. Prancing on my terrace in terror, ready to step out, doubting my decisions, the 'Anybody' for me then was my Rishi uncle, who reminded me, *"The world is your home now. Never forget that you can always return Home, back to your roots anytime and your family will be here for you."*

Simple words. Hopeful words. Kind words. It was the wind beneath my wings.

Different structures and practices of different times and cultures have enabled family members to build trust amongst them. In the older days, it was a natural sight of a row of women, oft times from different generations, oiling and/or braiding each other's hair and stories. Not only would one enjoy a good head massage but also a good massage to one's thoughts as conversations would naturally spring up. The quality of the conversations would depend upon the persons in the row.

I was always grateful to get a head massage from my grandmother's sister, my cousin grandmother, Kanta *nani*, who would ask me important questions of life. What is the meaning of life for you? What kind of quality of life do you wish for? What are you ready to do for it? I, in turn, felt safe to ask her some too. What have been your successes and failures in your life? What do you hope to achieve before you die?

I feel safe with some family members, more than with others. Yet, if we truly wish to cast the Indra net of relationships, one has to follow the beat of one's own heart to step up to build that relationship through conversations and silence.

So, what do we nurture in our silence and what do we say?

I hope and pray for you that you feel drawn to the beats of your truth in life. I trust you to practice the gift of deepening your relationships through dialogue, deep listening and designing ways to grow together.

Dreamily sending you blessings,

Grandma

PS: So, my lovely grandchildren, what are your stories of designing dreams to its destination for yourself and others as your *Practice of Satsang,* in your times?

"The best thing I can do for myself and the world is to have the courage to be myself, to find what I came here to do, then do it! We are all meant to shine, so shine bright, shine happy and shine free. You deserve to be you, the authentic, real you."

Iunia Pasca (2014)
(Rainbow Warrior,
Co-founded The Inner Spa, in Romania)

Now, it is time for Practice.
You may create your own or experiment with one I suggest below.

Practice
(D)

To be aware of your own beat of your heart. Designing the next step for change comes naturally when you are attuned to yourself.

Compose music for your life and family tree. There are many ways of doing this. I propose one, below.

- Use your body, or any materials as pots and pans, furniture and floor as percussion instruments. Create your own music for relationships that are fulfilling for you. Write on a piece of paper a line or two of gratitude for each of the persons.
- Create your music for relationships that you wish to work upon. Notice the difference in resonance from the music you created for the above. Yet, write a line or two of gratitude for each of the persons and also a line or two of what you hope to see in your relationship. Change the notes in your music and listen to it.
- Create more music for relationships that you have lost in your family tree that mattered to you. Listen for silence in it. Write a line or two of gratitude for each of the persons and also what you miss about her/him.

- What is the quality of your listening?
- Listen to your heart as you create music and see how it evolves – in a week, a month, a year, as you begin to take steps to design your future.

PS: It is helpful to do this with a loved one or two as you celebrate and contemplate.

PART
2

Practice of *Satsang* with Friends

Engine to take you across miles and smiles ~

~ Letters to my grandchildren ~

My dear little ones, out of the many words you will learn starting with the alphabet 'E', I have a few fundamental ones to share. In addition to 'Elephant' or 'Engineer', words that helped me to understand the world, the outer world, I was curious to gain access to the mysterious inner world that exists within us. The secret to peace, happiness and fulfillment lies in there. Our inner world determines how we respond to the outer world - people, places and perspectives. Practicing the essence of the few fundamental words below has been life-giving, nourishing and key to expanding possibilities for me.

As you grow each day into beautiful beings, I invite you to experiment, play and discover the essence of these words in your life. As you master the game, you will get clues to master your life and create your own future that is meaningful, day-by-day. The key is to choose wisely and practice consciously. Remember, whatever you practice; consciously, sub-consciously, or unconsciously, right or wrong, it grows stronger. So, what do you choose?

E for Empathy

- What has been your experience of feeling connected with another, understood by another, and not judged?
- What do you do or 'be' to connect with another, understand and not judge?

E for Enabling

- Who are you grateful to who has been the wind beneath your wings, helping the environment to be encouraging so you may fly higher?
- Who do you choose to support and encourage for their development?

E for Evolving and Energy

- What do you notice about the process of growth, evolution and change versus the state of stalemate or being stuck?
- What is your practice to attend to your energy and that of others?

Other words, also starting with 'E', also served me but only for short-term. Practice of the essence of these words fed my ego and exhausted me in the long-term as I found them to be life-depleting;

E for 'Egoistic', 'Evasive', and 'Enraged'.

Practice of *Satsang* with Friends – A Story

Engine to take you across miles and smiles ~

What is your engine to take you across miles with a smile during both good and bad times? Sure, there is the inner fuel; your inspiration, aspirations, values and virtues. Then there is the engine in different forms and shapes that show up in the form of friends and friendships.

So aek baar, a young girl from Assam dreamt of going to Mumbai. She may have been one amongst thousands, or is it millions and billions, who desire to go to the dream city of India. She worked towards getting admissions in the Tata Institute of Social Sciences, a Deemed University renowned for its work, research and outreach in Social Work. You have probably guessed who she is by now! She is none other than your adorable Assamese grandmother, Pinkie.

In that particular year in TISS, one would see a brown, furry, little ball of energy dashing from between the hostels to the classes to the Dining hall. Stay with me - I am talking about a dog-named Julie, who would frighten the day lights out of me! The other non-furry ball of energy that would protect me and assuage my fears was Pinkie!! I know, I cannot write about her with a straight face.

All of us in the hostel would unanimously bet that she had magical powers because we would see her in the Dining hall in one second and in the next second hear a friend screaming from the hostel room – we bet, at Pinkie! Surely, she must have met Harry Potter or some character from the series, perhaps Beatrix, we would lovingly tease her to learn the skills of teleporting herself. Infact, I do not remember seeing her walk, ever. She would run, dash, skip, hop, jump, roll – an absolute delight to watch on the badminton court. Each of those actions was accompanied with a special screech with and after the action.

The only time I ever saw her walking was on one very rainy, slippery day. Maybe she was with another friend and they were sharing an umbrella, so she had no choice. We crossed each other, faces half-hidden under the umbrellas. I ducked myself further but she still heard it.

The next day, after helping some of our visually-impaired friends with their homework, she walked over to me. She told me that she had seen a ghost walk up and down the lane with an umbrella the previous day in the rains. I looked at her – expressionless, with a complete poker face. Then she described animatedly how she had walked up and down, half-scared to bump into the ghost again. Her stories were accompanied with the apt hand gestures, facial expressions and a tone of voice that spoke of depth in the lightest manner possible. It was almost like watching a character come alive out of an animation movie. I started laughing. She continued describing her walk, how she was enjoying the rains, thinking of home, missing her family, Assamese food, the culture and all. In India, in the same country, culture, food, language can all vary to great lengths in the different States and Union Territories. It is almost like visiting a new country, when you travel from North-East to South-West or for that matter, in any other direction. I enjoyed listening to her articulating her emotions and immediately empathized. She must be yearning to connect and feel at home in Mumbai, I thought. I wanted to be there for her.

Finally, she looked straight at me in the eye and asked – "So, now tell me, why were you crying, you little ghost?" I blinked. I opened my mouth and shut it like a fish. It was such a huge relief to have your truth noticed by a friend, who creates a space for you to open into. I realized that she was the one who was empathizing with me all along and taking initiative in her own adorable way to ask if I were okay. She was articulating the intense feelings lightly that I was feeling but I could not bring myself to share with anyone. Why? Who would judge me? Surely, not her! I had a choice there – to step into the space and open up, or remain closed. Yet, I was afraid to be authentic. Yet again, I authentically wanted to be there for her, but how could I if I did not know how to be there for myself? I wanted to be there for her, but how could I if I did not show any signs of it, refused to be vulnerable, hid my emotions and myself behind a façade that 'I am Ok', 'everything is ok', when it was not!

You see the invaluable life lessons she taught me just by being herself, comfortable in her own weird skin, ready to empathise and willing to be real. I realized that many of my friends, including myself, face a dire situation. We are very willing to help others, but not necessarily, ourselves. We wish others to step into the space that we create but we tremble to take the first step. In denying ourselves, we forget that we reduce our capacity to help anyone. I often wondered when we learned consciously or sub-consciously that to be strong is to be emotionless. And if we refuse to be in touch with our emotions, does that make us into a robot society? What is the point of all the achievements if after all the successes we fail to be touch with ourselves?

What is life without a good friend even if you are in your dream city in the world? What is life with a good friend with whom one learns to wash away one's mask, one's pretense and relaxes into being that one really is, making life meaningful and purposeful?

That was only the beginning. Over time, Pinkie became an invitation for me to be authentic, open and the real me. We were very different in many ways and for many things, we would complement each other. It used to be like our breakfast before class begins, of bread and eggs, where she would want the yolk of both eggs and give me the two whites! We were lucky to have found each other! And as soon as I say this, I can almost hear her scowl and remind me that we have to work on our friendship too and that it evolves, with trust and with time. True enough, along the years, when she felt stuck and struggled to be authentic, I showed up as a remembrance for her. Guess that is why we need good old friends like good old wine.

Naturally, and because we were poles apart for the many day-day choices, we would get on to each other's nerves in a way that no one else could possibly compete with. At that stage of life, when one is trying to discover oneself and become self-aware, we helped each other in our evolution and understanding of ourselves by first, understanding the other and become other-aware! She would feel mild irritation every time I turned down an offer to go out so that I could work on an assignment to be submitted weeks down the line. 'Who does that?', she would incredulously ask and try to convince be that we had time by our side. Similarly, I would feel agitated to see her stress in the last minute, completing her assignments and rushing them out five minutes before the clock ticked its way to the deadline! All her running, jumping and screaming skills came in handy to even freeze time, as she would run to the Administration section to submit some of the hard copies.

'Why would you put yourself through that risk?', I would ask her hoping that she would plan and manage the next assignment better. She would just tell me how boring life is if you take no risk. We could never stop fretting at each other. She would not listen. She would not change. She would not learn and that would drive me up the wall. Of course, unbeknownst to her, I would be inspired by her and often turn the mirror inwards and look at my stubborn self. In my silent experiments, I would take small risks, try out what she offered at the other end of the spectrum but would never admit to her that I was learning from her, not until much later after our Graduation!

Until then, we would have our epic mock fights, mercilessly teasing each other, ganging up with other friends and protecting each one's version of the story. Yet, at the heart of it, we knew that we could trust each other. We knew that the feedback given was healthy and coming from a good place, even though we chose not to listen to it, overtly. Covertly, however, we deeply appreciated the other for who she was. That made us a great team! In our first group assignment, it was a wonder that murder was not reported in the papers! After we got through the storm of mutually finding a date to meet up, not too early, and not too close to the deadline, discuss and plan, we realized that we were a great team. I worked on the bits required to make the base before the deadline and she completed it incorporating last minute interviews and perspectives till the deadline. We had to admit to each other's strengths.

Why does one stray away from being authentic and put on masks in new circles and situations? I am tempted to generalize this - Always, people have an innate need to belong, to fit in a group, to be liked and end up with varying behaviours to meet that goal. It is natural for everyone to wish to feel in harmony and in peace within and without, in his or her own friend's circles or diverse circles.

I remember I had shown up as myself in all-varying colours in a friends' circle of 4 friends before Mumbai that had attracted the wrath of the group, who had unanimously decided to 'break up' with me. It has been heart breaking to see my girl friends walk away, leaving me alone. I was aware of the mistakes I had made and the cost that I had to pay for it. I was naturally afraid in the new college, in the new city, amongst new 'friends'. Yet, if I were not my natural self, who else could I be? Pinkie turned out to be a true friend who helped me see that.

I had tried to fit the norm, but my self-expression in thoughts, words and actions could not be hid. It was a learning curve to accept myself, feel centered, feel safe and be a friend to myself before I could be a friend to another. It was a learning curve to not to judge myself just as I would learn not to judge others. It is easy not to judge others once you get to know their story and where they are coming from. Pinkie, and other amazing friendships sprouted in that college year that could be harvested even years later.

Look at your past. Look closely at your friends you have picked in different ages and stages of your life. Or, did they pick you? What are the gifts you see in your energies as you relate to each other? What are the lessons learnt and how do they contribute towards growth for everyone, as each one of you evolves, in varying speed and directions? Have you forgiven yourself and others for things in the past and let by gone be by gone? Or are you carrying the old agreements till date? Do you need to clean and take care of your engine? When is the last time you celebrated an old friendship?

'Friendship' for me, has changed over the years. Seeing who I hang out with is a good indication of who I have been as a person in different stages of my life. In my restricted, safe Primary school days, friendship was just a bunch of classmates from the same community in the neighbourhood. We would go to school together in the bus, study, play, fight, and compete in studies against each other. If someone fell ill, we would reluctantly share the school notes with the other's parent! We were only allowed an annual visit to our friends' homes; to attend their birthday party, eat the cake, give and receive presents in exchange, and go home before it got too late.

I was envious to know of how 'Friendship' for some people in certain cities from their school days was to stay over at each other's homes, cook together, read, play, travel and join extra-curricular activities. At the same time, it was more humbling to know how 'Friendship' for yet few others was to befriend God by praying for the safety of one's family and friends. They grew up in an unsafe environment to the sound of gunshots in certain parts of the county. It puts one's life in perspective for sure.

I recalled a childhood incident when life was indeed put in perspective for my earliest bunch of school friends. Learning to empathise was a shocking lesson for us. One day, I had walked with eager feet to the bus stop. The bus stop used to be the place to play because by the time we would reach school, it used to be class time! It was a bright, sunny day. I smiled as I saw my friends from the neighbourhood cross the street, though it waned away when I looked at their ash-stricken faces. They were cousins and even before they could cross the street completely, they spilled out that one of our friends (and their cousin) had met with an accident, going face-down in a pot of frying dish – She was in the hospital with severe burns.

'Is it possible that something like this can happen in real life?', our naïve, innocent, young adolescent selves asked. We were shocked. We heard the story over and over again until the shriek of the school bell silenced us. During lunch, we gathered together to wonder if she was ok. Those days, we did not have any cell phones, so it was all speculation. How long would it be before she could completely recover? How painful might that have been? For the first time, to my delicate memory, we articulated our fears, our questions, our thoughts, instead of quarreling, comparing and competing – something that we learnt from a young age – wonder how!

Something shifted for all of us. We send our best wishes to our friend. We committed to help though we did not know how. I readily wanted to share my class notes. Time passed. I still remember the tinge of 'ouch, that must have been so painful, God, please help her' feeling in my heart when I saw her after she returned to school. It was the first time I had ever prayed that earnestly for her. For once, my thoughts and prayers were all for her than for myself. Turning my thoughts today to her, she is doing great as an accomplished lady today, taking care of her husband, her family, her career, her friends and all. Thank goodness for Facebook to get in touch with all other school friends, as we become friends anew, evolving from what we used to be.

Self-awareness gives cues to manage one-self. Becoming aware of the other's personality, needs, strengths and styles give cues to manage the relationship between the two people involved. The fire of friendship can be awakened any time, with any one, as long as you are willing to share your inner fuel to oil the engine to cross miles, be it in the real world or the virtual world.

Sure, one has to be vigilant and discrete as fire can be both constructive and destructive. Even while it is burning bright, one has to attend to it and not take it for granted. Yet, a pure fire would have lasting warmth amongst friends to pick up from where they left off, even after months or years of meeting up. It is indeed a blessed joy to meet an old friend, almost like visiting your own younger version of the self trying to climb a tree, and be witnessed by the same friend sitting calmly under the tree, or maybe, atop the tree, or even planting new trees!

I have felt blessed in my life as I meet every now and then old friends from school, college and work-life. We remind each other what a different version we used to be like so-an-so V1.0, who has now become V30.0! For some, the Intel is the same yet there has been improvement. Confidence shared is confidence multiplied.

I had lost touch with Pinkie for years in between as we each focused on things that we were attending to in our respective busy lives. Then one day, we got in touch with each other with no baggage for not being in touch for so long. We realized we would soon enter our thirty's and leave the twenty's behind! Her birthday was approaching. She was dreading that. As she was sharing her feelings with me over the phone, my mind drifted as I was hit by a brain-wave. It was the perfect reason, not that we needed one but maybe we did (when did we learn that we have to justify things to ourselves?), for her to make a trip to Singapore. We had to celebrate this.

Expecting nothing to have changed, I was pleasantly shocked when she got her passport, visa, and tickets in place way before the deadline! She actually planned out her trip, well. Waiting for her at the airport, I saw a brown, furry, little bag, on four wheels whizz by me. It was a dainty lady's bag carried by a gorgeous lady, who was none other than Pinkie! I could hardly recognize her. What we did recognize was new friction firing its way between us as we tried to box each other in the old 'her' and 'me'. Soon we could not stop laughing as we paused to see the new versions of each other. Accepting our new selves, we got to know each other anew. Feeling refueled in our energies, and re-connecting, we had a memorable holiday. Before we knew it, she used those teleporting skills of hers that I had always suspected to go back.

Yet, going back is sometimes going forward as we could rely on each other's engines to move us from stuck moods towards constructive choices in the times ahead. All it took was one phone call, one message, and one unabashed shout – help!

I hope and pray for you that you find your reliable engines in your inner world and in your relationships in life. I trust you to practice that which would enable you and others to evolve and expand your energies to serve the world.

Enjoy my dears,

Grandma

P.S. So, my lovely grandchildren, what are your stories of enabling, empathizing and embodying trust, as your *Practice of Satsang,* in your times?

"Arrgghh! You and your philosophy!!! Your grandchildren would be relieved that you are resting in peace! …but… they would not know what a precious gem they are missing out on."

Pinkie Borgoyari (2013)
-(Civil Servant, Assam)

(Warning: do not quote the above,
it takes finesse to get away
without being hurt!)

Now, it is time for Practice.
You may create your own or experiment with one I suggest below.

Practice
(E)

To be aware of your evolution over the years of who you show up as in circles and in friendships. It is an invitation to celebrate the work-in-progress that you are.

- Make your own life mandala depicting the various stages of life from which you have evolved. Accessories needed: paper, paint, crayons etc.
- Paint the masquerade party corner with all the masks you still hold on to.
- Paint the letting-go corner with all the masks that you have left behind.
- Paint the engines depicting each friend - the person one has grown into and all that you know that has shaped her or his ways of thinking, relating and doing.
- Paint the paths and tracks that have served you well, that lie broken, that are mending and new ones that you wish to travel on further.

PS: Be creative. Go wild. Use props. Enjoy and do it with a group of close friends or by yourself, whichever may be your preference.

Fun is the new Fine ~

~ Letters to my grandchildren ~

My dear little ones, out of the many words you will learn starting with the alphabet 'F', I have a few fundamental ones to share. In addition to 'Fruit' or 'Flower', words that helped me to understand the world, the outer world, I was curious to gain access to the mysterious inner world that exists within us. The secret to peace, happiness and fulfillment lies in there. Our inner world determines how we respond to the outer world - people, places and perspectives. Practicing the essence of the few fundamental words below has been life-giving, nourishing and key to expanding possibilities for me.

As you grow each day into beautiful beings, I invite you to experiment, play and discover the essence of these words in your life. As you master the game, you will get clues to master your life and create your own future that is meaningful, day-by-day. The key is to choose wisely and practice consciously. Remember, whatever you practice; consciously, sub-consciously, or unconsciously, right or wrong, it grows stronger. So, what do you choose?

F for 'Freedom'

- What are the qualities you discover to taste freedom and take ownership of your free, truest, best self?
- What do you do or not do to enable others discover their freedom?

F for 'Feedback' or 'Feed-Forward' with yourself and with others

- What do you admire and learn from those who give you true, even difficult, feedback with appreciation and compassion so you may grow fully unto your best self?
- What is your core from which you seek and give feedback?

F for 'Forgiveness'

- What does it feel like to be truly forgiven when you are intentionally and truly sorry for your words or actions?
- What do you practice to completely forgive yourself and the other?

Other words, also starting with 'F', also served me but only for short-term. Practice of the essence of these words fed my ego and exhausted me in the long-term as I found them to be life-depleting;

F for 'Fearful', 'Forceful', and 'Fake'.

Practice of *Satsang* with Friends – A Story

Fun is the new Fine ~

So, I was in the 'fine city', where I saw T-shirts and signage of warnings; 'No urinating in the lift', 'No spitting', 'No smoking', 'No water wasting', 'No chewing gum', 'No dumping' and so on and so forth. Instead of raising taxes, the Indian and some other governments ought to learn from Singapore and impose such fines!

A diverse bunch of us were in Singapore at the same time thanks to AIESEC for our internships. We had our own inner system for fines for friends from different nationalities, diverse cultures and dynamic personalities. If we would get the facts and figures of each other's countries and cultures wrong, we were forced to learn their AIESEC national roll call – a string of acrobatic dance moves and lyrics woven together, ranging from ultra crazy to pure insanity. Or, we had to fulfill a dare and step up to face our own fears. Or, we had to contribute by introducing something meaningful from our own culture/ ethnicity. Never before had I learnt about the geography of places, the history of individuals and their families during the World Wars, the economics of economies of various countries through personal stories. I was always grateful for my bunch of friends in India and we had learnt much, experientially, about each other's region, language and culture. The world just expanded with friends from faraway lands!

Food, almost always, is one of the first areas of high impact. We tasted delicacies and new tastes of international dishes that we had never even heard of before. Fun is another prominent area. We got introduced to art, culture and movies in different languages with translations. We would have our own mini international movie and food festivals, each one bringing something special from their region. The Bollywood nights would be the longest, doubtlessly, with a follow-up with some necessary dancing and singing.

AIESEC is an international youth non-profit organization that provides students leadership training and internship opportunities for profit and non-profit organisations and communities. The key is that it is a student driven organization committed to fulfillment of humankind's potential, starting with youth. It is firmly based on the principles of empowerment, practice, innovation and care. Some of us used to warmly coin it as 'epic' tuning in to favourite soap opera character! More of the description can be found on the website about the world's largest youth organisation and the incredible story of its humble roots during the times of world war. If you are keen to play the role of a listener, ask any AIESECER what the experience brought to them in their life and then sit back to enjoy the heartfelt stories.

I still recall one of the powerful evenings where we watched 'Schindler's list'. We were a group of different nationalities in the room – Austrian, Estonian, Russian, Chinese, Japanese, Columbian, Indian, Pakistani, Egyptian, Singaporean, Hungarian, Kenyan and Hong Kong. After the movie, some shared how their grandparents were forced to participate in the war, sometimes even the same family's brothers was divided and distributed in different enemies' camps. Others shared their reality of growing up in an environment as part of the Communist regime and what a different world we are living into. One of the friends had seen and tasted fruits in the tropical island country, Singapore for the very first time in her life!

They emphasized the need for world peace, and the small piece each one of us can play, fired by their personal stories. We also learnt of the Chinese, Japanese and Singaporean history in the Asian and Global context. The Indian and Pakistani shared their common history in an uncommon way that would rarely be read in any publications. It was the best History lesson I had ever attended where I actually began to feel compassion and caring for something bigger than us. History suddenly had a purpose, to feed forward and for the existing generation to make the desired changes.

Also, later in the years, when the Egyptian revolution took place, we actually heard firsthand stories from our 'Egyptian King' friend, Hazem and his wife, Lina, from Egypt, in addition to the ones through social and conventional media. We had them and our Egyptian-Singaporean friend, Yasmine, join the protests. Waves of changes, voices, protests is still reverberating our planet as our generation connects with social media in ways that was not possible in the past. Many of us get our news from Facebook first than the news channels.

We also begin to see and hear what the media does not cover. A stark existing example is that of 'Rosia Montana', where the ambition to create Europe's largest open-cast gold mine by blasting away four mountains, grinding down the rock and soaking it in 240.000 tons of cyanide was shared with us by our Romanian friends, who were there joining the protests to save communities, heritage and environment.

One cannot help but feel connected with what happens across the globe when you have friends who are in that situation, whose families get affected and they give the perspective that is otherwise inaccessible!

One often undermines one's own power and contribution to things that seem big, and way out of one's circle of influence and impact. Just by the virtue of good friendships, I learnt about the power of my power to support a friend across borders. One of the biggest gifts is to listen to their stories and uplift their spirit so that they can uplift the spirit of the ones on the ground directly.

Friends bring lightness and flexibility to rigid memories. It used to be a hoot when we would compare the English pronunciation of any one word in various accents. Of course, it used to be a delight to see the American and Australian/ British friends argue dramatically over spellings of words in the English language. The rest of us would happily blame them for all the confusion between 'color' and 'colour', 'organisation' and 'organization'. It was a catharsis for those friends who did not do well in their English papers at school. It was the best cross-cultural lesson we ever had with a balance between learning, teasing, understanding and appreciating the reality or worldview of the other.

Mostly, I learnt a deeper lesson of life – to trust the imagination of youth and enable them to build capabilities to not just earn a living in life but to live life in a way that would help pay forward kindly and compassionately. I vowed to remember this lesson even as my youth days passed by. Be careful if you accept naysayers' views or conform too quickly. Let your inner compass be your guide and find friends who can help realize your dreams, even as you help them realize theirs.

These were few gifts of AIESEC. It created an opportunity for youths from diverse walks of life to meet, stay together, work together, and build on resilient friendships that would hopefully last long after the university journey, internship and AIESEC experience. It is very experiential and for any mistake, fun seems to be the new fine. There are ample training and learning opportunities in AIESEC to get new awareness, sharpen one's skills and build on a new domain. It is one of those organisations where the mistakes are forgiven and balanced with ample mentoring. The punishment is to co-own and co-create ideally, balancing between one's own learning curve and the organisation's performing curve. Friends, aka your colleagues, support you.

It also created an opportunity for youths to leave their homes or homelands in relatively safe ways and to stay overseas, experiencing work-life, a fine life!

It is both an experience and a learning to stay with 2-3 different nationalities. The kitchen is a micro representative of a global super market with various spices, coffee and ingredients. Never mind the faux pas in cooking and mixing different spices! One of my most shocking experiences is mistaking the Japanese cuisine's wasabi to be some Indian innocent mint chutney and having a mouthful of it! Ouch!!!

The living room is a micro representative of a global conference where diversity thrives, local music from faraway lands throb and you begin to get a gist of unfamiliar languages. Amidst all the chaos, there was always one anchor, one unanimous point-of-view. Why do we need to iron our clothes? Who made that rule in this history of humankind? If I were to generalize one human aspect, it would be that every single one, without fail, does not like/hates ironing clothes. In all houses, the living room's corner with the ironing board held testimony to that as whoever went to that space would either wail or be grumpy. It was not so fine!

Learning was a big theme for some of us. We wanted to practice with friends to sharpen our presentation skills and content knowledge of various subjects that each one was introduced to in the work place. For a period of about two years, Sunday was not about going to church but going to the living room prepared to make a presentation. We had all graduated from internship to getting full time jobs as trainers in different organisations. Struggling in the initial deep waters at work, a natural ritual emerged to gather for brunch but before that to earn it by practising floundering to flawless presentations. Of course everyone tried his or her best to present. And then came the challenging part – to give feedback. One of our friends taught us about feed-forward; to give feedback that enables a person to move forward constructively. We also discussed the various feedback models out there in the market and experienced them all by trial-and-error.

The worst and later on, the best circles were those where we could give open, honest feedback to each other. Feedback is one of those experiences that cannot be dished out unless there is trust in the relationship. And when we do have trust, is it still natural to be afraid of giving authentic feedback? What are we afraid of? Is it losing the friend, hurting the person or becoming the unpopular person? If we truly care about another, in all circles, it is essential to have a structure and process of giving/receiving balanced feedback.

I recalled how in earlier days, without a feedback loop, good friends chose to house together because after all they were good friends. However, best of friends do not necessarily automatically make the best of flat mates. Many lost their trust because of failure to communicate one's needs, one's preferences and understand where the other was coming from. The cost was high. Spite, jealousy and misunderstanding invited colossal amounts of wastage of one's energy that was life draining for everyone involved. The loop holes could be simple day-to-day habits as not replacing food taken out from the stores, using another's favourite cup/spoon, keeping the house dirty, stepping onto each other's boundaries etc. Some houses had had scenes similar to that of Big House, the reality TV show! Thus, the lesson was well learnt – to always look out for the feedback loop for learning.

Another feedback loop is to notice new patterns in different stages of life. One glaring one emerged for us soon after a few months of getting into our new jobs.

We forgot about learning when we began to concentrate on earning. We forgot fun!

Not only that, we lost precious much. Every time we met any of the friends, there was a fresh bout of complaints about the new job, boss, colleagues and clients. It was universal with the exception of a select few. Soon, the edge of the diversity rubbed off as the system turned to one big, complaining, giant mess – about doing too much, in too little time, with too little support and motivation, getting too little pay packages or incentives.

Over a period of time, friends began to feel tired, sick and it became a chore to meet each other. We called it the process of age-ing! Who were we? What were we becoming? We thought we were done with that phase in the teenage years but guess it comes once in every decade – for some, sooner, for some, later. In those times of chaos and confusion, underneath the seeming complaints, there was an urgent search for meaning. Some of the primary questions floating around were: 'Where do I fit and belong?', 'What is my passion?', 'Who am I becoming as a person leaving my family behind and creating my life in a new country?', 'What can I do to take care of my family who is back at home?', 'What do I want from life?' and the ever-famous, 'Who am I?' I was swimming in the same pool with others, diving in similar quests.

As friends, one gets the privilege to listen to one's deepest hopes and aspirations and even fears and limitations. How could we support each others' ideas, enable each other to take action on them and make it worthwhile for friends to meet up and enjoy evenings like we used to (without complaining!)

A coincidental conversation with my friend, whom you would know as your Belgian grandfather, Andries De Vos, gave me a clue. He shared with us about a practice of inquiry and discovery that Andries had learnt in Europe. It is called Pro-Action café. It is a process that encourages participation from people to bring their ideas into action through support of the community.

Like the name, it intends to have a cafeteria or informal setting with people sharing their ideas that they wish to implement, listening to each other and asking or giving support. Unlike in a Barista or real cafeteria, there is a host and a process that supports and allows the flow of a generative conversation guided through powerful questions to turn ideas to action.

With a clear purpose to have safe spaces where people could come together to have a dialogue around those questions, freely express their doubts and dreams, seek resources, ideas and help from others; we gave birth to the monthly Singapore version of Pro-Action café; a participatory methodology where every person attending it is both a speaker and audience. Compare this to a conventional formal conference where you are only the audience and the others are experts. People are invited in these evenings to take responsibility for one's passion and choose to be passionate about one's responsibility.

Few members in the audience step up to choose the topic that they want to talk about. The others can choose the conversation they wish to sit in for and choose to listen or share or ask good questions. By the end of the evenings, strangers would become friends as they shared their stories from their lives, their experiences and their ideas. Not only that, some even teamed up to gather resources and help each other. In my times, this was not a common practice – wonder how is it in your times?

I fondly remember those evenings where we would meet just the core group of friends/hosts to plan for the main evenings. We were creatively wild in our ideas, learning to partner with each other and getting to know of each other's strengths and fears. When anyone did well, we would celebrate the joy. When anyone messed up, we would step up to support. When anyone was afraid, we would challenge – sometimes gently, sometimes not so! We learnt about freedom to be ourselves and let others be too. We learnt to forgive for sharp remarks, ouch moments and embarrassing moments. We learnt to have fun and faith in ourselves, in each other and in the many new friends we made each time we met – some for short-term, some for longer.

It was fun. It was sacred moments of our lives. It helped bring out the sacredness in each one of us in our own unique ways.

It was one of the most synchronic, organic creations by the friends, for the friends and we did befriend hundreds of others from diverse fields in the three years that I practiced this. It was a great story of learning across borders as the methodology was co-created by Ria Beck and Rainer von Leoprechting – your great-parents, who are practitioners of social technologies and generative dialogue practices, teaching many change agents the same.

I have heard stories of many a TEDx event and other social platforms and even some business platforms have been created with the same ingredients of synchronicity, friendship, curiosity and purpose. Do any of these sound familiar to you in your times? We only hoped that after the war era, surviving era, striving era, we created practices that would lead to a thriving era in which you would live. One of the biggest lessons in doing something, versus reading about it or just living in the world of ideas was the experience of flying emotions. I love the phrase – have your skin in the game to make it real and meaningful.

Even sacred moments are forgotten. One has to be conscious about them.

It was interesting how after a while, we realized that the serpent of complaining had entered even in this volunteering creation between friends. 'Feedback' – this was the most difficult of the lot to practice that led to holding back of emotions, resentment, resignation and complaining! Complying to peer pressure is the easier route out.

After more than a year of practice, though everybody enjoyed hosting the main evenings, not everybody was as committed to attending to the energy behind the scenes and in planning for the event. Some did not feel appreciated enough. Some did not feel engaged enough. Some had adapted to the patterns and were not reading the cues for change. After a while, there was enough accumulation of ouch moments when each one of us wanted to share what we thought and how we felt but were afraid to hurt each other.

In pure fun, we were able to evoke the sacred best in each other in the past. In pure routine, fun was replaced with angst, worry in the absence of honest feedback.

So, we held a pro-action café on the theme of 'feedback'. To my biased memory, this was the most powerful café. We explored some good questions –

Why is it easy to give appreciative, good feedback but not difficult, constructive feedback even amongst close friends? Is that shallow? If we continue to do this, are we truly supporting each other in growth and learning? (Some people do the opposite – comfortable in giving harsh feedback with no compassion, so the person receiving the feedback has no idea about one's strengths. Speak the truth in giving feedback but not all of the truth needs to be spoken in one serving that would leave the other feel bruised and battered with no integration of learning. One can help scope the feedback by asking what is true, necessary and kind.)

- Are you someone who actively asks for feedback? Does it make it easier to give feedback if people occasionally ask for it? Are you at least someone who accepts the feedback given to you as something worth considering?
- There may be times when one is not ready for any kind of feedback. As close friends, how do we read the timing to be right?
- You can imagine, in the conversation of exploring these questions, we ended up giving each other feedback that revealed blind spots with real-life examples. Everyone felt relieved and more connected. There was trust, space to lean on each other and feel validated, affirmed and loved and learn from the mistakes.

Something powerful had shifted for all of us. Something got unlocked and unblocked in that session. Even years afterwards, when we are all in different countries, it is still so easy to give and receive feedback even on Skype. It has become a ritual for all the grandmothers to meet on Skype and do an informal Pro-action Café. We end up peer coaching, offering support, love and authentic feedback. We are like giraffes watching each others' backs.

I hope and pray for you that you find your unique bunch of fun, passionate friends who will watch your back and give you feedback on your face, out of love and care for your way forward. I trust you to practice constantly carving the path of freedom, forgiveness and fearlessness in your inner world and in your relationships in life.

Fly high my dears,

Grandma

PS: So, my lovely grandchildren, what are your stories of fun times, forgiving times, freeing times and feedback times as your *Practice of Satsang*, in your times?

"Do it. Do it not for what you will get but for who you will become."

-Hui Min Toh (2014)
-(Coach & Happy Woman)

She went on an AIESEC internship to Finland
And *Initiated Pro Action Café there. Yay!*

*"What principles of living and material are you
dealing with in your live and work?"*

-Rainer von Leoprechting (2014)
-(Pro Action Café co-founder & creator
of powerful processes for organisations)

He gifted me this question to travel with in his farm, Obenaus in Austria,
As he and Lena Jakobsson graciously hosted my stay there in my sabbatical.

Now, it is time for Practice.
You may create your own or experiment with one I suggest below.

Practice
(F)

To be aware of feedback loops in your life. Find examples in your life that
naturally tends to give feedback and make you self - aware.

- Notice the natural examples in day-to-day life:
  o Sharp cut by a knife in the kitchen if used carelessly – What does that
    tell you about being in the present versus mentally drifting?
  o Weighing scale – What does that tell you about your patterns and
    choices of food intake, physical activities and overall well-being?

o   Health scans or fear to go for one – What does fear teach you? What is your thought pattern that reinforces the fear or get freedom from fear?

o   Find the right friend to share your problem and chart out ways to get out of it, toward the fulfillment of mutual dreams.

- Be the friend who does not judge another even if you hear of say, an illicit relationship or choice that you yourself would never undertake. Even when it goes against your values, how can you practice sharing the truth lovingly and kindly by judging the action but not your friend?

PS: Value fun.

Growing Forests ~

~ Letters to my grandchildren ~

My dear little ones, out of the many words you will learn starting with the alphabet 'G', I have a few fundamental ones to share. In addition to 'Goat' or 'Goal', words that helped me to understand the world, the outer world, I was curious to gain access to the mysterious inner world that exists within us. The secret to peace, happiness and fulfillment lies in there. Our inner world determines how we respond to the outer world - people, places and perspectives. Practicing the essence of the few fundamental words below has been life-giving, nourishing and key to expanding possibilities for me.

As you grow each day into beautiful beings, I invite you to experiment, play and discover the essence of these words in your life. As you master the game, you will get clues to master your life and create your own future that is meaningful, day-by-day. The key is to choose wisely and practice consciously. Remember, whatever you practice; consciously, sub-consciously, or unconsciously, right or wrong, it grows stronger. So, what do you choose?

G for Gravity and Groundedness

- What is your relationship with the universal law of gravity, bringing steadiness and groundedness in life?
- What is your sacred ground on which you relate to others?

G for Gratitude

- What is your colour of gratitude that paints your life, each day?
- What kaleidoscope appears as you graciously feel gratitude for small and big things, towards people, opportunities and challenges?

G for Generosity

- What is it like when others are generous towards you with their time, energy, resources and spirit?

- What do you do to cultivate generosity in yourself for yourself, others and the environment?

Other words, also starting with 'G', also served me but only for short-term. Practice of the essence of these words fed my ego and exhausted me in the long-term as I found them to be life-depleting;

G for 'Guilt - trips', 'Gloomy' and 'Grumpy'.

Practice of *Satsang* with Friends – A Story

Growing Forests ~

Do you remember the first person in your life with whom you shared about your first crush, the fluttering of the heart, the experience of blushing? Did you and that friend break into giggles and gentle musings? Did you enjoy the teasing thereafter? Through life's innocent nuances as such, many learn to create a special, sacred space, which allows you to experience the opening of hearts. Be it in laughter and mirth, or sorrow and sadness, it is essential to have a friend/s who gives you that space to open your heart. It may or may not be logical. It may or may not be right, or wrong. It is just as it is - recognition!

That sacred space if shared with a family member, and reciprocated well, galvanizes into friendship and grows into a strong, reliable bond. This is for all parents who wish to be friends with their children and wonder how. Creating that sacred space with one's child allows parents to have a dialogue around family and cultural values. The sacred space allows questions on love and romance, sex and sexuality to thrive, doubt to dissipate, faith to blossom and trust to develop in the parent-child relationship. Awareness and mindfulness about relationships is cultivated and nurtured. Even when children and parents go afar physically, the beauty of it draws children back to the parents, back in the sacred space, in the hour of need.

After all, there is just one tiny difference between sacred and scared!

What is the difference between crush and love?

Who can forget the inevitable teasing of crushes, special attentions, and imaginary incidents in school life? My school friends and I were all gifted writers, at least scriptwriters, irrespective of how one performed in the language papers, with innovative fairy-tales for each other. We could have contributed myriad scripts to Bollywood, though maybe many stories were inspired from that source and the songs itself. Your Bengali grandmother, Jayita and I did a fun, informal survey where we found out that in a bus of perhaps 150 High school girls from an all-girls-school, the primary conversations going on were about crush, ideal love, life partners and those 'annoying boys' from the all-boys-school in the town.

The dreaming and distractions would intensify especially around Inter-school competitions which was the only time we would go to the all-boys school, and for many that was the only real experience of meeting the boys. Needless to say, both as participants or supporters, we would put on our best fierce competitor suits, and return not only with victories of trophies but also with many interesting stories of victories over hearts! Those were the days when we would fly, far away from the ground, in the vast expansive sky of imagination and musings. It was all naïve and fun play. Examinations, reality and few friends centered on career dreams would help ground the others.

Before one could blink an eye, school days got over. It is a small town and this was the last century. Parents began to speak of marriage. Many of us wanted to continue our education. Different friends had different reactions and responses towards arranged marriages, staying or leaving the town for further studies, choice of subjects, colleges, breaking hearts or fulfilling dreams. Many were rooted in family values, personal values and were clear on the path ahead. Everyone was in the same eco-system, getting influenced by each other and trying to influence each other. Always divided and recognized by the four school teams and colors, we began to divide ourselves into Shakespeare's four humors in our philosophy of leading our lives: melancholic, phlegmatic, choleric and sanguine!

Those days were the last of when I spoke to your Bengali grandmothers, who were cousins and my best buddies in High school, Chandrabali and Oindrila, as we all went to different Metropolitan cities to study. Life continued as college life took over.

One fine day, out of the blue, I got a call from Chandrabali inviting me to her wedding in Kolkata. Her marriage was arranged with an engineer who lived in the States. The call was a surprise as we had not spoken to each other for ages but the news was not. It was expected, sooner or later, to receive an invitation for an arranged marriage at that age. She was one of the first few friends in the batch to get married. I felt awful that I could not attend her wedding or meet her before she left the country. I remembered all our conversations about our dreams for the ideal man and hoped that her dreams had come true. Then I went back to living my life.

Life was too short, too busy, too focused as Oindrila and I evaded marriage to pursue our dreams of securing a job. As luck would have it, we found ourselves in the same city, Mumbai, after a few years of separation and silence. It is a boon to have an old school friend in a different stage of life. They are powerful mirrors of the increasing growth or gap in who you used to be and who are you growing to be? We rekindled our sacred space of sharing, exploring and celebrating life. We were grateful to have our dreams fulfilled and enter work lives – something our respective mothers could not do but had supported us so that we may break the pattern.

Chandrabali had also broken a pattern, meanwhile. Something, that none of us would have suspected her capable of doing so. Something, that nobody in her family had done so. However, this is the thing about breaking patterns. Depending on subjective factors, cultural values, some patterns when broken are celebrated whilst other patterns when broken are frowned upon. Truth be told, for all cases, there would be a fragment of people who would be frowning and another fragment of people who would be celebrating. So, it depends if the fragment of people that matters to you is your family, what are their response, understanding and appreciation to your brave act of breaking a pattern?

Chandrabali had made a bold choice and chosen the path of divorce. She was back in India, back in our small town. Oindrila and I would get together and wonder how she was coping with it all. We knew coming from the background that we did that this was indeed a very big step that needed courage and choice. We knew that her choice may not be welcomed by many. I had not had the chance to talk to her for years by then. There were a lot of unknowns then. We did not know the root of her reasons. We did not know how long she had been struggling with this, all by herself. We did not know what life had in store for her, or for ourselves for that matter. All we knew was that she was facing a lot of resistance to grow that young shoot of divorce, uprooting herself from the secure, tall, thriving idea tree of marriage!

The news was akin to a forest fire, crackling its way across. It threatened to turn to ashes the tiny shoot of divorce even as the process was underway. It was a tough time for her and her family in a forest where the norm was that of arranged marriages, sticking to it and making the best out of it. After all, our parent's generation had more severe arranged marriage rules. Rules are made for a reason too. Not all forest fires are bad. They are part of nature. There is a lesson to be learnt. It cracked open conversations in many families that were resistant to address matters earlier and hoped that things would just be and continue to be. Real conversations began to take place about the sacredness of marriage. Of course all our parents hoped that none of us would have to go through the process of divorce in our lifetime.

Oindrila connected with her mother, responding responsibly to her family trials. She is the first in her family to go for a love marriage. I remember re-kindling my sacred space on the phone with my mother, who lived in that same forest (our families were neighbours) in the same ecosystem of norms, 'shoulds' and 'musts'. But there are always different species even in the same ecosystem. My mother had taught me to appreciate that diversity.

Chandrabali was not getting much appreciation for her perspective and her choice. She was caught feeling strangled in the web amongst questions and suggestions, guilt and fear. Some of the family's well-wishers got together to help and decided to send her to Mumbai. Oindrila and I were ecstatic. We had a plan. We picked her up from the airport, and sat talking an entire weekend. Finally, we knew what was to be known. We cried. We laughed. We planned. We chastised her and loved her. It was reminiscent of school days except then the biggest problem was to do well in exams. This was the examination of life and we shared notes to ace it.

Soon life unfolded as per all our hopes. Chandrabali got a job. We spend precious couple of years thereafter in Mumbai. It was many a magical weekend, where we would meet, cook, celebrate and live life to the fullest, still wondering about love and life and grateful for the generosity of friendship that had tied us again. We were nurturing new trees rooted to the old ones.

Life goes on. I had left Mumbai and again, had not created a chance to talk to Chandrabali for months. We did not hold any grudge on that. We had faith in our friendship by then.

Then, one day, out of the blue, I got a call from her inviting me to her wedding. Her marriage was arranged with an engineer who lived in the States! Déjà vu! This call was a big surprise. Our minds love patterns and I ended up sharing my concern just as many others had done so, wondering if she were impulsive, if she had thought this through etcetra. She was prepared and responded confidently and caringly. I suddenly felt ashamed that instead of inquiring, I was jumping the gun, digging the past pattern and giving my advice, as if I were the expert! I grounded myself instantly to be with what was growing, then, and suspend my judgment.

Seasons change.

Today, Chandrabali travels between India and the States. Following the law of positive phototropism, she and her family had grown towards the light source with strengthened roots, healthier shoots and abundant fruits.

I had a chance to meet her and her husband when I traveled home. We spent a good evening eating our favourite local foods, enjoying old and new conversations, co-creating a sacred space amidst us. When she and I had some alone time together, I finally had the chance to understand the details of her story. Seeing her grounded, centered, happy and willing to work towards what matters, I walked away grateful for our relationship that survived the fire of judgment and jumping to conclusions, without knowing her story.

Every real relationship has to undergo different seasons and stand strong in all of them. The learning continues. Life continues. Life is just beautiful when you have a friend indeed, whom you turn to in need. Life is just magical if you have more than a friend and family members, parents and siblings are also your true friends. Reversely, are you a special friend like that to someone too who turns to you? Often, some people can give and do not know how to receive. Again, some people can receive and do not know how to give. How can you balance the generosity?

I hope and pray for you that you thrive in growing forests in your inner world and in your relationships in life. I trust you to make choices when you are feeling grounded, grateful and generous for yourself and others.

Rootedly rooting for you,

Grandma

PS: So, my lovely grandchildren, what is your love story that you hope for? Whatever might be the journey, how might you uproot those roots that serve no more with gratitude for having taught the lessons it did and ground the roots of values and virtues to serve beyond your lifetime, for your *Practice of Satsang*, in your times?

"See the best in the worst of situations and stay true to yourself".

-Chandrabali Maitra (2013)
-(Soul traveller)

"Taking a decision is easy. It is learning to live with the consequences, which is difficult. Happy learning""

-Oindrila Maitra (2013)
-(Legal Counsel)

Now, it is time for Practice.
You may create your own or experiment with one I suggest below.

Practice
(G)

To feel grounded, stable, calm and centered. There are diverse ways. Enjoy playing with different ideas and see which one works for you.

- Take a lesson or two on gardening in the real world, not the Farmville or other versions in the virtual world.
- Take care of a pet; pat a dog, bring milk for the cat, care for a horse.
- Pray.
- Watch the stars. Listen to the ocean. Enjoy the sun-rise and sun-set.
- Breathe slowly inhaling gratitude and generosity and exhaling stress.
- Feel roots growing from your feet into the ground, connecting with other roots and feel yourself growing towards the light.
- Listen to nature inside you and outside you. It is one.
- Feel loved and protected.

PS: Love and protect.

Hatching and living a dream with Honour ~

~ Letters to my grandchildren ~

My dear little ones, out of the many words you will learn starting with the alphabet 'H', I have a few fundamental ones to share. In addition to 'Hat' or 'Heart', words that helped me to understand the world, the outer world, I was curious to gain access to the mysterious inner world that exists within us. The secret to peace, happiness and fulfillment lies in there. Our inner world determines how we respond to the outer world - people, places and perspectives. Practicing the essence of the few fundamental words below has been life-giving, nourishing and key to expanding possibilities for me.

As you grow each day into beautiful beings, I invite you to experiment, play and discover the essence of these words in your life. As you master the game, you will get clues to master your life and create your own future that is meaningful, day-by-day. The key is to choose wisely and practice consciously. Remember, whatever you practice; consciously, sub-consciously, or unconsciously, right or wrong, it grows stronger. So, what do you choose?

H for Hope and Happiness

- What is your experience of hope and happiness at the brightest and darkest hours?
- What do you do or not do to remind others of the same gifts?

H for Habit of Health, Healing and Harmony

- What does it feel like to be healthy in body, mind and spirit, letting go of old wounds and letting in of harmony and healing?
- What do you practice to feel holistically healthy?

H for Helping and Seeking Help with Humility

- What do you admire about those who request for help when needed and give what they can with humility?

- What is your core from which you seek and give help to humanity?

Other words, also starting with 'H', also served me but only for short-term. Practice of the essence of these words fed my ego and exhausted me in the long-term as I found them to be life-depleting;

H for 'Helpless', 'Hopeless', and 'Hostile'.

Practice of *Satsang* with Friends – A Story

Hatching and living a dream with Honour ~

People always spoke of hope and happiness. Governments take surveys of which nations are happy or happier. I would always wonder what does hope and happiness look like. It changed from having an ice-cream with the family, to playing games accompanied with squeals, to enjoying a drink with friends, to sitting and staring at the sky, to studying and teaching self and others, to having a job, having friends, having a special someone, to traveling, to volunteering, to learning a new skill, to sitting with questions that matter and reflecting amidst the busyness of life!

The invention of cell phones, change in life-style with reliance on Skype, mails, new media, initially triggered off a wave of connectivity with friends from far-away shores. Staying in touch in meaningful ways became a possibility without having to traveling miles and synchronizing calendars. Albeit over time, we wondered if we were even in touch with ourselves as there were phases of life when nothing could make one happy, when I caught myself living life meaninglessly and aimlessly.

Does that ever happen to you? Hmm!

Good old friends are sometimes the best to turn to when in doubt. One such evening, over a general 'catch-up' with four more girlfriends, the conversation steered towards wishes and dreams in life. If you have friends who are coaches, inevitably the conversation turns to that of powerful questions.

'Have you experienced moments when you truly do not know what is it that you wish for?', somebody asked.

'What is the point in knowing? Heck! Ignorance is bliss.'

'You are saying that! Did you have a bad day?'

'Maybe we just need to learn to live with not knowing. I am tired of trying.'

'Whoa! I hear frustration.'

Yes! It is so frustrating. If we do not know, who else will? How do you get to the place of knowing with certainty? I was lost in my inner dialogue when I heard a dreamy voice, 'When you are frustrated, ask yourself one thing you know and you will be surprised by the answer as I was – I know that I want to learn horse-riding' said someone at the table.

Horse-riding! Oh hell, yeah! As if we were in a Transformers' movie, the mood changed. Within the blink of an eye, there were three more 'yes' agreements. The mood shifted. It turned from a somber, casual and some-what reflective one to one of action and planning. I found myself party to the planning of the possibilities with gusto, while sharing stories of the few experiences I had had in Darjeeling and in North India, listening to other experiences from Hungary, Romania and Philippines. Also synchronicity helped. I knew of a friend who would go for horse-riding lessons to Malaysia and knew of a package that was possible for all of us.

Within a few minutes, we had a plan in place. As things started to shape up, we took a deep breath of satisfaction as there was something to look forward to. Calming down, we realized that only four of us had agreed and that there was a quiet somebody, listening intently to us. We all turned to look at her with raised eyebrows.

"I can't believe all of you are already planning for this and actually, have come up with a plan which is incredible within a few minutes! Learning Horse-riding has been a child-hood dream for me!" She said that in a shocked-like state. We were confused. Why was she the quietest and the most silent of us all then? It did not make sense. That was your Singaporean grandmother and my friend, Vani, known for her love for learning, adept in the world of Mathematics, logic, literature arts – we would call her Versatile Vani!

Her quiet, intense energy threw us all off-guard. How could she be quiet? If it were me and my childhood dream, I would be jumping up with joy at the first opportunity and leading the plan. Little did we realize then how much it meant to her to have what seemed as a fairy-tale fantasy actually being even articulated out loud! It was a dream she had held on to for hope in some dire moments in her life. It was a dream to imagine herself galloping across the greens on a horseback. It was a dream that meant much to her and seemed so far away from reality, from ever coming true that she could not believe her ears when she heard one of us speak of her dream. She expected the rest of us to laugh at the ridiculousness of the idea at that voice. She was surprised, no, shocked, when she saw us jump at the opportunity and take the insane idea seriously. She had always imagined others to laugh at her dream of horse riding, or discourage her from doing such an un-practical thing! She was told at time that she was living in a parallel world. It all seemed so unrealistic and surreal to her.

Have you ever been afraid of articulating your dreams? Have you ever been ridiculed for your dreams? Have you ridiculed others for their dreams, because it sounds silly, impossible and improbable?

We learnt a powerful lesson that day of how even as friends when we tease each other, our innate judgments and comments can sometimes have the potential of killing others' dreams and hopes. Even naïve but constant teasing someone about their height, weight, skin color, accent, looks, habits, stamina reinforces the belief in the other person's mind that she or he is not good enough. It is worthwhile to reflect if you are a friend who creates a space of opportunity and hope or a space of ridicule and hopeless reality?

Vani shared her story, which was different from any of my friends. She and her brothers had to drop out of school when they were 11, 10 and nine years old, leaving Singapore to live in India. For the next seven years, they moved back and forth between India and Singapore almost every year living in six different homes where money was never constant and every aspiration shot down and ridiculed. Passionate about learning and determined to get an education as the path to a life of freedom, Vani studied on her own by reading textbooks. Arriving back in Singapore, she finally persuaded her parents to let her attend the last two years of high school, which allowed her to catch up and go to university and eventually to lead an independent life. But this difficult experience had made her cautious and timid; hopes and dreams were a source of vulnerability, opening her to disappointment and heartache, so she gave up and kept her head down to focus on just surviving and getting by. She had never thought that her childhood dream ever had the possibility of coming true!

We grinned wide.

What were friends for after all, if not to share your craziest dreams with?

She could not believe her eyes and all other senses when just a fortnight from that evening, the whole bunch of us traveled to Malaysia, spending a weekend with horses. I could not believe myself when I thoroughly enjoyed the experience. At the end of that weekend, we gathered around the dinner table to give space to the loudest and the quietest of voices for the gifts they both bring. We wondered aloud how many times in life instead of choosing to create our own happiness and hopefully sharing our ideas with good friends, we choose to stay silent for fear of our own self-limiting thoughts. After all, what is the purpose of good friends if they cannot so much as entertain one's hopes and aspirations?

To Vani's credit, she visited that ranch every weekend for months afterwards and learnt horse-riding well. It gave her the confidence to dare to pursue her other dreams that had been hidden away. With much perseverance, she moved to Geneva, Switzerland, to continue her studies overseas as she had dreamt, at the Graduate Institute of International and Development Studies, and work in a field she was passionate about, helping others who are disadvantaged so that they could have the same opportunities that she had to struggle for.

The horse-riding story brought forth sharing of many other friends who had wanted to experience scuba-diving, sky-diving, learn a foreign language, cook a new dish, run a marathon – 10 KM, 21 KM, 42 KM, meditate, write a book, go for further studies, play the piano or the cello or inculcate a new habit/hobby. I discretely remember how the conversations visibly shifted amidst friends where there were real conversations around problems. Instead of getting stuck in the game of blaming, feeling helpless and hopeless, it was very satisfying to dive into dialogue with a purpose of creating solutions or capacity to deal with the problems.

I discretely remember how I shifted in my inner world from a world of self-limiting thoughts to a world of possibilities after making the same mistake of ridiculing an idea. I could not stop myself from guffawing when my friend and your Indian grandfather, Srujan said that he was going to the Everest Base Camp! Of course I justified that I had my reasons for my reservation. He was skinny, an engineer, a nerd Egyptology student and would begin to pant if he climbed as much as twenty stairs! I learnt to heed the voice of reason from a constructive place when he prepared and surprised us all by making his dream come true. He would fondly recall how he and his buddy were the only two Indians in a pool of Americans and Eurasians climbing the sacred paths to Mt Everest.

None of us had climbed a mountain except for the occasional trek. He had expanded our worldview to explore this new thought of climbing mountains! In his entire lineage, he was the first one to have done so. After his wedding, he took his wife to climb Mt Fuji in Japan for their honeymoon! He encouraged his friends also and soon enough, I found myself with another mutual friend at the summit of Mt.Kinabalu in Borneo (East Malaysia) in 2011. This was not even on my bucket list!

Indeed, it became possible to create a new culture, create new consciousness and create new bucket lists in one's circle. It became possible to observe old-mental barriers that were limiting us to recognize our full potential. This was in sync with stories we heard of from friends from other circles. One of them send a powerful article of facilitating conversations among families from Israel and Palestine, who boldly and honestly shared their pains of being victims to mankind's war of power and struggle on both sides. But instead of charging their pain and stories to create more violence, they advocated changing those stories to create spaces of sharing the lessons and think of ideas of lasting peace for the coming generations. They wished for them to be healed of and freed from the pain their great-grandparents had experienced.

Like outgoing ripples of water, we learnt that personal peace enhances peace in one's circles, peace in the community, the nation and amidst generations and nations. One can however appreciate and care about the larger game of harmony and humanity when one has play-mates for one's personal game of humility and healthiness and heartiness.

I hope and pray for you that you hatch the very dreams that you are afraid of and live a life of honour. I trust you to practice ways that beget harmony for optimum health in your inner world and in your relationships.

Heartily hugging you,

Grandma

PS: So, my lovely grandchildren, what are you stories of helping, healing and having hope for yourself and others as your *Practice of Satsang,* in your times?

"The simplest, even the most clichéd words, take on a more profound meaning when heard at the right time. 'You never know what you could do until you try', my professor said to me when I had thought I had made the biggest mistake of my life in taking on something that was beyond my capacity but somehow I had survived and even succeeded. My hands were shaking and I was on the verge of tears, having had too little sleep and too much fear for too many days but I was struck still by these words as if they had been a spell. I felt a sudden clarity and lightness. I had been underestimating myself, playing small, keeping myself safe in a tiny space that eventually started to feel like my tomb. You have more courage, fortitude and resilience than you think you do. The path you desire may be not easy but it is within your capability once you commit to it."

-Kalaivani Karunanethy (2014)
-(*Vani*, Life-long Learner)

Now, it is time for Practice.
You may create your own or experiment with one I suggest below.

Practice
(H)

To recognize and work towards the fulfillment of your dreams.

- Make a bucket list of dreams that you wish to fulfill. Remember to leave some space for dreams that you may not have thought of, so far.
- Share the bucket list with family members and friends who matter. Read their bucket lists and listen to their dreams.
- Pick one dream. Take the first step.

PS: Remember to revisit your bucket list frequently. Also, it is ok to drop some items off the list when you feel it is the best thing to do so. Feel complete.

PART 3

Practice of *Satsang* with Fellow Travellers

Impossible possibilities in creating desired Identities ~

~ Letters to my grandchildren ~

My dear little ones, out of the many words you will learn starting with the alphabet 'I', I have a few fundamental ones to share. In addition to 'Ice-cream' or 'iPhone', words that helped me to understand the world, the outer world, I was curious to gain access to the mysterious inner world that exists within us. The secret to peace, happiness and fulfillment lies in there. Our inner world determines how we respond to the outer world - people, places and perspectives. Practicing the essence of the few fundamental words below has been life-giving, nourishing and key to expanding possibilities for me.

As you grow each day into beautiful beings, I invite you to experiment, play and discover the essence of these words in your life. As you master the game, you will get clues to master your life and create your own future that is meaningful, day-by-day. The key is to choose wisely and practice consciously. Remember, whatever you practice; consciously, sub-consciously, or unconsciously, right or wrong, it grows stronger. So, what do you choose?

I for Intentions

- What have you observed about people who have clarity of intent, who work towards realising it before starting the journey and keeps a check on it during the journey, even if it means taking a longer scenic route?
- What do you practice to clarify your intent?

I for Imagine, Innovate and Inspire

- What have been the colours, shapes and subjects of imagination and innovation that has left you inspired?
- What do you observe for yourself the difference between real and imagined worlds and what do you practice inch by inch to bring it together?

I for Integrity

- What is a person with integrity for you?
- What are your integral practices to be and feel the whole of mind, body and spirit?

Other words, still starting with 'A', also served me but only for short-term. Practice of the essence of these words fed my ego and exhausted me in the long-term as I found them to be life-depleting;

I for 'Impatience', 'Intimidation' and 'Incongruence'.

Practice of *Satsang* with Fellow Travellers – A Story

Impossible possibilities in creating desired Identities ~

What is your story of 'aek baar......' that you recall as a memorable conversation with a far-away-friend or stranger if you will, who listened to you, said something that stayed with you, made you reflect, unlocked a stuck thought for you? I have often heard people say that sometimes a stranger, by virtue of strangeness, is able to address something that your family and friends cannot.

In the world with its share of safe and unsafe people, one has to be discerning about one's contact with strangers. That is why, I like the term, fellow travellers. My construct of fellow travellers are people whom you meet in safer places as perhaps conferences and similar learning spaces of the field one is interest in or in a friend's house or when you bump into someone separated by six degrees of separation and so on and so forth. Fellow travellers may end up being your good friends in the long run. Or, they may be people you keep in touch with once in a while. Or, they may even be people from your field of work and play, whom you admire.

It is a thin line to define who truly is a fellow-traveller? Technically, everybody is a fellow-traveller, traversing this lifetime with us. Practically, one comes across many strangers in many different settings, with different intentions. With new media and the virtual world expanding, this opened up a world of possibilities; of hope and danger. The key is to feel the pulse of the emerging worlds and stay attuned.

In my times today, virtual media enables such connectivity through LinkedIn, Twitter, Google Circles. Wonder by your times, what else might become possible?

It was such a far cry from older times. Your great-great-great grandmother had a beautiful ability and style to connect with strangers in the trains, in the marketplaces, in the doctor's chamber while awaiting her turn. In those times, there would be thriving conversations. It was the way of life. She was known to be the lady who would listen well, leave behind a food for thought, a ray of hope, a memory for the soul with strangers and non-strangers, irrespective of meeting them again or not.

Over generations, the trains, the marketplaces, the chambers changed where that level of interaction was not visible. Perhaps it is the people who changed. Perhaps it is the people, who when fearful of the changing world encouraged their young ones not to talk to strangers. Sometimes, that was useful advice too. Your great-grandfather was actually given food with sleeping pills in the train once and clean-shaved of his goods that he was carrying for business. Thus, it is difficult for parents to guide their young ones. Everyone has to develop their instinctive levels of discretion. With lack of discretion, one can also go to the other extreme and become absolutely closed and fearful. Some choose to be safe than sorry with strangers and even fellow travelers, and also friends and family!

In the real world too, I only realized the wealth of perspectives I could learn from fellow-travelers when I made amazing friends out of strangers in workshops and courses, as these were safer, constructive spaces where many came with intentions to learn. One of the effective ones was a course to build capacity in counseling by Dr. Minnu Bhonsle in Heart to Heart Counseling Center in Mumbai. Her process of training was to allow conversations amongst the course mates rather than just learn theory or listen to experts alone. We had to practice unmasking our true selves in front of our mates. That allowed us to see each other in deeper varying shades than just the surface monotone colors which we proudly differentiated ourselves with. I found it unique to experience a different reality of a person when I listened to her/him than the reality I had created in my mind for her/him in my own head!

This became an invaluable lesson for me that helped me much to connect with many strangers in the future. Instead of putting people in boxes, the minute I have one label for them, I learnt to listen to their answers and interpretations. I learnt to listen to what they were not articulating. It is priceless to learn this, even in the face of other people putting you in boxes. People put people in boxes. People create structures that reinforce this mental model. One of the easiest structures is to look at the administrative forms one has to fill in with close-ended questions.

I definitely learnt labels and boxes anew when I traveled. In Singapore, one time, when I was filling up a form, there was a box termed 'Race'. I stood stupefied. The only corollary to 'race' I could think of in that moment was a 'marathon'! I knew that the form was not asking a question about sports. In that panic, I did not know the answer to the question, 'what is my race?' (OMG!!!). (Yes, you can call me naïve and laugh at me!) Embarrassed, I turned to the officer to ask, "So, what race am I, do you know?" It was the first time that day in my life that I realized and more importantly, internalized that my race is Indian. As a piece of knowledge, I had always known the answer. As a place of consciousness, I could not equate race to Indian, perhaps because there is much consciousness around religious differences in India. In Singapore, the same is also for race. The four nationally recognized categories of races in Singapore are Chinese, Malays, Indians and Others. There are Singaporean Indians, whose race is Indian but nationality is Singaporean. Their religions can differ from Hinduism, Islam, Buddhism or other. It gets more interesting for children born to couples from mixed races, faiths, nationalities etc. The simple question of 'where are you from' begets a complex answer.

Was it really that complex? I had to learn about this new world (or the same world that you begin to see with new eyes), these new distinctions, the identities that held meaning for people, the identities that were forced by others on people for the sake of segregation. My friends chastised me telling me it was not that different from India where we had caste system and cultural ethnicities etcetra. It was very confusing for a foreigner to understand all this in India. A French friend piped up how all of these distinctions based on race and religion would be considered illegal in France.

The world was changing, had changed from my grandparent's generation to mine and bet it will not be the same in your times. The question was how does one learn about the world matters? What source does one trust?

I have learnt of the wisdom of researching through the layers of complexity. It is worthwhile to look at the personal sources and stories as much as it is necessary to see what national and international sources of news portray.

An example: India-Pakistan tensions, Hindu-Muslim differences, 1947 split! I read the story in History books and learnt about the separations, the violence, the pain, neighbours killing neighbours etc. I listened to the news from archives and documentaries and movies and the trickling aftermath stirring more hatred, intolerance, war and impact of that incident to my times. I also heard it firsthand that my Hindu paternal grandparents had escaped in the partition because of the help of their Muslim friends. My paternal grandmother (*dadima*) had worn a 'burqa' then that had saved her life and lives today to see her future generations and tell the story. Various sources – variety of answers – variant choices, the question is what do you choose to believe and which story do you wish to populate?

As I have shared, I had a safe space to explore the sources, the perspectives, the varying shades in dialogue with my parents. I saw them change like work-in-progress, even as I was changing. Curious about others, I was heartened when I heard the story of a fellow-traveler from Iran, your great-great grandmother, my teacher and a fellow-traveler, Mojgan, who created those safe spaces not only for her family, but for many other fellow travellers seeking to find answers and growth in Singapore, along with her husband.

Born in the family with a grandfather whose identity was Muslim, she witnessed the change in her grandparents as they not only converted to the Baha'I faith, but also became the founder of the practice. Stories of persecution of the followers of the faith in Iran are heard even today. Turning into her teens, she loved the encouragement to independently investigate her own interpretation of the faith. She took her time to toil her inner land of values, build her own muscles of spiritual reflections and questions in the face of life's opportunities and difficulties. She had lost her parents at the young age of four, had to travel to stay with different family members with her brother, and was wandering and wondering about identity.

Growing up, she chose to continue to be a practitioner of the Baha'I faith. She believed in exploring inter-faith possibilities, equality of men and women as the Baha'i faith espouses, even when it all seemed impossible. She and her husband, Mehrdad have opened the doors to their home to host friends and strangers with dinner and a safe space to reflect on topics and questions that matter. She is known to be a teacher with a difference. She continues to learn. She trained herself to be a facilitator of the Virtues Project, where the emphasis was to practice one's faith and higher ideals through virtues. With the need of character development and values in 21st century education worldwide, she did her bit professionally, serving through workshops held for parents, children and teachers to enable building their muscles of reflections, dialogue and practice of one's virtues. This was the differentiator. Personal life can rarely be different from professional self, for a learner as her.

I was one such stranger, who met her at a time when I was in the centre of a storm in my life. Just attending her 'Reflections' evenings, meeting many other like-minded, international and diverse fellow-travelers, I found my center of calmness and faith in toiling in my inner land, the mind. Guess that is how I realized we are all permanent drafts indeed and it is our choices and intentions that make who we are.

History is full of examples of wars world-wide and we are in perpetual mystery of inner conflicts, questions and battles. There is indeed much to learn from the past. The question is what do we choose to learn to create a meaningful future?

For many of the foreigners, living in Singapore, the multitude of religion, race, Asian identities, and diversity was very interesting and complex. I must admit my horizons expanded too as I got to know of faiths/religions/practices I had not even heard of!

For this I have to thank my Pro-Action friend, and your Mauritian grandfather, Jovin, who was also a facilitator volunteering in many circles. He invited me to attend one Sunday morning, an Inter-Faith Dialogue. "What is that?" I asked incredulously.

'It is an informal, friendly platform where people from different faiths gather to talk about their perspectives from their faiths. To ensure that it remains as a dialogue and not a theological debate, we as facilitators choose a topic and through questions, invite personal sharing on it. This month's topic is 'Faith and Sustainability", Jovin replied. He also explained how this Explorations-in-Faith, fondly called E-i-F was stewarded by South East CDC, Singapore Government's conscious attempts to educate its people to have religious harmony in the Island-Country. That was in 2009.

I went. I met many interesting fellow-travelers, young and old. They were locals and foreigners, first-timers and many-timers. They were from different faiths and no-faiths. Some called themselves atheists, agnostics, free-thinkers, spiritual seekers than attach themselves to any faith. Some just preferred to call themselves, 'explorer', 'searcher', 'researcher', and 'wonderer' even if they were Hindus, Muslims, Christians, Buddhists, Taoists or Baha'is in the forms one fills, probably because the forms do not give these other categories the space.

It was a memorable first-time experience for me. There were curious and challenging questions, logical, historical and emotive perspectives, and stories from personal lenses. One of the ground rules that I liked much was that anything any individual said, was not representative of his/her religious body. It was a personal comment because no one was speaking in the capacity of a religious leader (even if religious leaders were present too). It made people responsible in the way they spoke based on their understanding, belief, practice from a personal lens. The conversations were truly generative even between a Father of a church and an Imam, a father of two teenagers from an Inter-faith marriage and a young person, me. It was representative of multi-generational and multi-cultural dialogue. It was a true satsang ~ the search for truth, understanding and appreciation of truth, where people could speak their own truths. It was like a lego playing field in my brain. So many possibilities!

The question was, was this sustainable out of that safe space?

What makes a safe space between strangers for authentic dialogue? Whose responsibility is it to create that?

Dancing in the questions, I met many fellow dancers, living and working to create innovative solutions to the same question. One of my earliest teachers and friend is Farid Hamid, the master-trainer-of-facilitators of these safe spaces. He is known to have sown many a seed to flourish in the garden of inter-faith dialogues in Singapore. He also nourished many a sapling to grow in the garden of Explorations-in- Ethnicity by One People Singapore where I learnt much about races, social identities and personal identities. Farid, similar to Mojgan and other admirable teachers attended to many plants and weeds, firstly in his own mind and heart. Responding to a true calling of peaceful sacredness, he lives a conscious life enabling the creation of spaces for others to grow and 'garden' too.

It was the stories that he shared from his personal struggles, choices he made that filled the pages of his life, dreams he wished to write in the empty pages that made me realize the obvious – of course, one cannot teach dance unless one dances. There was no escape for me. If I intended to truly learn, I had to put on my dancing shoes and jump into the ring with other fellow-travelers.

Meanwhile, remarkable fellow travellers and mates were dancing all across in Singapore; again, young and old, foreigners and locals. I found myself in a 'new discotheque'. Since 2009 till date, I have seen the many diverse fellow travellers serve the larger purpose of working as worker bees towards the honey of world peace through creating safe spaces for dialogue, through contributing with the best of what they have and through connecting with more and more fellow travelers in the process.

There was the 'dancing lessons' – Circle Conversations hosted by Al-Nandhah mosque in Bishan where I learnt much from Guat.

There was the 'dancing lessons' offered by the government.

There was the 'dancing lessons' created, experimented, shared by ground-up initiatives and individuals.

There was the healthy dance between believers and cynics. There were still the violent dances in life where incidents of intolerance took place nonetheless. There was the dance of rising consciousness and articulation in form of protests, Facebook Pages and causes in the virtual world too.

When I got tired of dancing and sat down to rest for months and months on end, consciously choosing not to connect with any of my circles of fellow travelers, they continued to dance and welcomed me instantly when I wanted to return. I learnt the invaluable lessons of true faith in the goodness of humanity then.

I hope and pray for you that you feel assured in your explorations of impossible possibilities in creating desired identities. I trust you to practice being a learner in search of truth, truthful to virtues of peace and joy needed for humanity to thrive.

Imagine,

Grandma

PS: So, my lovely grandchildren, what are your stories of meeting people and perspectives with imagination and innovation than right and wrong attitude as your *Practice of Satsang*, in your times?

"Struggle each day to serve humanity, practising a virtue that will help create a better world for our grandchildren."

-Mojgan (2013)
(Soul Teacher)

Now, it is time for Practice.
You may create your own or experiment with one I suggest below.

Practice
(I)

To practice expanding your horizons around faith, race and other forms of social identities that divides and separates.

- Visit a place of worship (of your own faith or that of another faith, where appropriate) with an open heart (alone or with a friend/fellow traveller).
- Invite a friend or fellow traveller to visit your place of worship or your sacred space and share what meaning it holds for you.
- Investigate the truth of an identity and the meaning held with an open mind and listening ear. Go deep to find the source of truth than to swim in shallow waters.

PS: Pick a virtue or value as Love or Peacefulness to guide through the experience of expanding your horizon and stretching out of your comfort zone.

Journeys with Meaning ~

~ Letters to my grandchildren ~

My dear little ones, out of the many words you will learn starting with the alphabet 'J', I have a few fundamental ones to share. In addition to 'Jam' or 'Jeep', words that helped me to understand the world, the outer world, I was curious to gain access to the mysterious inner world that exists within us. The secret to peace, happiness and fulfillment lies in there. Our inner world determines how we respond to the outer world - people, places and perspectives. Practicing the essence of the few fundamental words below has been life-giving, nourishing and key to expanding possibilities for me.

As you grow each day into beautiful beings, I invite you to experiment, play and discover the essence of these words in your life. As you master the game, you will get clues to master your life and create your own future that is meaningful, day-by-day. The key is to choose wisely and practice consciously. Remember, whatever you practice; consciously, sub-consciously, or unconsciously, right or wrong, it grows stronger. So, what do you choose?

J for Joy

- What are moments of Joy that you have cherished?
- What is required to make the choice to be joyful and spread joy for others, both in good and bad times?

J for Just and Justice

- What is your internal locus of justice based on – values, virtues, humanity, learning or punishment, biases, rules?
- What do you choose to stand up for in life?

J for Jambo! (Jambo means "Hello" in Swahili)

- What is your curiosity and learning about the spirit of people speaking languages different from you and coming from cultures?

- What is your personal contribution in sharing about your own meaningful practices with others in an invitational way?

Other words, still starting with 'J', also served me but only for short-term. Practice of the essence of these words fed my ego and exhausted me in the long-term as I found them to be life-depleting;

J for 'Jealousy', 'Judgmental' and 'Jaded'.

Practice of *Satsang* with Fellow Travelers – A Story

Journeys with Meaning ~

What is your first memory of travelling?

I read this question in a travel blog and got lost in my memory lane. I have seen photographs of me as a child with my parents in Nepal but I have no recollection of it. My first thought is that of waiting in the car as our car was stopped for customary inspection at the border area between Nepal and India. A group of brown clothes, which later I was told were policemen's costumes, came to check if we had brought anything from Nepal. We had. They took away a big doll called 'Shanky' that I was holding. It was nothing compared to the Barbie dolls that came up later on. It was a cloth doll dressed in red, smart clothes and there was pink somewhere on it (was it the hair or the nose?) that had mesmerized me. I was three or four years old then.

They took my Shanky away from me. My father accompanied them to the brown shack in the corner. My eyes followed the pink color and before anyone knew it, I managed to stumble out of the car on my own and followed my father to get my Shanky back. When I was not paid any attention, I started to cry and cried until one of the policemen came running to me with Shankie and gave it to me, speaking soft, soothing words that sounded gibberish to me. I instantly quietened down, hugged my Shanky and returned to the car. I vaguely recall father saying that they did not return the chocolates and biscuits. My aunt, who had brought those chocolates and biscuits, wryly said that if I had cried for them too, maybe we would get it back. I had learnt my lesson: when you want something that is meaningful to you, take the first step.

What is your favourite travel destination so far? Why do some places stand out more than others do? When does a place, or the memory of it become meaningful for you? Is it because of the people or the place itself? Or, is it because something within you changed, or came to awareness, when you were there? What is that special something you bring back home from such a place?

Is it materialistic, or is it a transforming 'you', who begins to sustain and share the peace and the joy felt in the holiday period, even after the holidays?

I have met fellow-travelers who enjoy the art of traveling from an entire spectrum; the beginners and amateurs, the professionals, the curious, the travel addicts, the adventurous, the pensive, the real, the virtual, the want-to's but life happens while they are still making plans. Wonder how would you describe yourself! This list is not exhaustive and one can be a combination of various versions too.

One of the most enticing conversations with fellow travellers is around the art of traveling. People express the art through photographs, stories, insights and observations. Some are open to experience the different sensations, irrespective of whether they like it or not. The key is that it is different and real. They try out the local cuisines, immerse in the local cultures, meet the locals to understand and appreciate the place, its history and its people more. Others are not so open for various reasons that matter to them and search for similar sensations of what one is used to back home. Again, some are open in their minds and hearts for new learning in the inner world even if they may not be as experimental with the physical world.

Facebook allowed for sharing of travel moments in unique ways. Every now and then a comment would pop up in any of the travel photos of anyone, 'I am jealous!' Friends learnt to manage their jealousy and soon encouraged each other to become travel buddies. After all, jealousy is just an emotion that screams with clarity of what you want. Sometimes, it is about things that you want but cannot have. True friends would just help you discover alternate ways to go about working towards your dreams and moving away from the emotion of jealousy. In my times, travel became one of the most opportune collaborations amidst friends and fellow travellers.

It made me reflect on the opportunities I created or lost when I travel. My nature of traveling changed, initially, my style was just rushed trips where everything is planned on an itinerary to the dot, irrespective of whether I am part of a group, or alone. It used to be a thrill to visit the tourist places, take photographs, and rush to the next one for more photographs. I only felt fulfilled, then, to cover as much as possible. Later on, it became more experiential to immerse in the activities be it sky-diving, scuba diving or other that was out of my comfort zone. Adrenaline can be an addiction. I would not allow any addiction after its short span of time. So, yes, it changed again. Soon after, I sought places with nature that offered a possibility to lose oneself in or find oneself. I sought experiences of a relaxed, meaningful conversation over *chai* with the locals, or with traveling companions, or family. My friends teased me that it was a sign of growing old. Perhaps it was, but it changed, yet again. I began to travel to places where friends lived to see that part of the world from their eyes. Sometimes it coincided with their weddings and celebrations adding further meaning to the travel plan. My art of traveling soon became a hybrid of sorts, and there were no right and wrong ways, just conscious choices.

What is a journey with meaning?

What is a journey with meaning, for you?

This was a question that a fellow traveler, Vinod, was contemplating upon for himself. As a musician and composer, an avid reader and facilitator, he found himself drawn to invite more people in dialogue and action of living a conscious life. I met him in the virtual world years ago. Mubashira, my co-research buddy from university connected us. Like the thousands of connections in the virtual world, this one had the danger of slipping by after a courtesy mail. But something about inquiring into life and practice, Vinod and I continued to stay in touch.

That is when I discovered that he hosts learning journeys to Leh, Ladakh, called 'Journeys with Meaning'. In Vinod's own words, "there's travel. And then there's...travel that transforms you. It wraps seductive new ideas & perspectives around your head, shaking out the older, outdated ways of thinking you've been carrying around for years. When you're looking but not really seeing, it thumps you unpolitely on the back of the head demanding that you see past the camera lens into the essence of a place, asking you to listen carefully to the ancient stories hidden within every tree and under every rock."

I imagined if I had met Vinod in my phase of travel and photography, he might be the one to thump me 'unpolitely' on the back of my head stuck to the camera lens! Luckily enough, I had changed and by the time I met him, his travel itinerary offered exactly what I was looking for.

His invitation for Leh was for 15 days traversing through the gorgeous landscape, stay in home-stay, stay in the tents in the wilderness, visit the monasteries, trek and white water rafting. It has the combination of balancing adrenaline gushes with possibilities of quiet hushes with oneself or with nature. I wanted to sign up for the travel, but 15 days! Who has 15 days to spend in the same place on vacation, an old thought within me questioned? But Ladakh is one of those places that cannot be rushed to suit the convenience of city travelers. One needs the required days to acclimatize and truly experience the place. While the city-girl in me still had her doubts, the mountain-girl in me found a way to take out 15 days out of the city life of work and responsibilities and signed up. I took the first step.

I arrived in Kashmir. It has been Mubashira's dream that one day, more and more people would feel safe to travel to Kashmir. Sitting on Dal Lake in a houseboat, sipping on *kahwa* tea, writing these very letters to you even then, I met the rest of the group of fellow travellers for the first time. They were healers, social workers, a mid-wife, designers, youth in between college and work, and those between work, and those who needed a break from work. All in all, it consisted of individuals open to question their lives and explore. Perfect!

It was more than just travelling and a journey indeed. We stayed up drinking more *chai* and conversing about the social, political and economic state of the state. We learnt much as we listened to the stories of the locals conversing with the crew of the houseboat too. Waking up at dawn, some of us visited the floating market and were reminded that we were tourists. We forgot about that as we spend nine-ten hours on the road for two straight days to reach Leh. We learnt much about each other, about Kargil and other places we crossed past. I forgot my city-life impulse of reaching my destination as fast as possible. I was actually enjoying the journey by road.

The mountains, the passes, the scenery gripped my heart. The fellow travellers gripped my focus as we exchanged stories, empowering resources on development, sustainability and change along the way.

The journey was definitely conscious traveling as the fellow travellers shared tips on reducing waste and respecting the space. We were all armed with steel water bottles to avoid the purchase and throw of plastic water bottles. We were eagerly awaiting to meet the local entrepreneurship in the town of Leh where they charged a minimal amount to fill up those steel water bottles than to sell only plastic bottles of water. We shared notes on carbon footprint, simple ways to reduce, recycle and regenerate and before we knew it, we had reached Leh.

Once in Leh, we had a home stay. In my times, Couch Surfing had made this very popular in many cities across borders. In the small town of Leh, this was a way of life to host travellers who came from far-away villages. With its growing popularity, a bevy of hotels and inns had opened up and the younger generations were soon forgetting about hosting and home-stays. To keep that tradition alive, Vinod had purposefully collaborated with the local friends there to give us a more realistic experience of every-day life in Leh.

Using the dry compost toilets which are specially made as a response to save water and attuning to the environment there was a novelty experience. We witnessed the truth of the locals, who were hard working, striving to survive in an other-wise harsh environment, attending to their gardens, their families, their livelihood but with a smile on their lips and a shine in their eyes that came from a deep spiritual source.

They were friendly to the workers who came from all over India during the summers and did their best to host their guests. Drinking lot of *chai,* they never hesitated to offer one with a biscuit and a story. In that space, time seemed to relax too. Almost never punctual, much to the chagrin of some city guests, Leh offered the possibilities of appreciating an organic way of life for many of us in the group.

Journeys with Meaning, which is what Vinod had coined his offering was indeed one. Not only did we have enough time for ourselves, for each other, for the markets and the musings of the travellers but also we had enough time to visit NGOs and villages. It was a polite thump, I would dare say, to listen to the stories from different generations of locals there. I was truly intrigued by the efforts put into education and preservation of the local flora and fauna. The local children shared how they grew up reading about the tiger, giraffe, elephants in their text books but listened to the stories of the bharal (Himalayan blue sheep), the snow leopard and the need to protect their cattle from the latter's attack.

I got to know of more fellow travellers then whom I would never meet in life but shared a truth with them nonetheless. I met them in the tucked away corners and book stores of the markets and the monasteries. Peter Matthiessen, who just passed away a few days ago, was one such fellow traveller who accompanied me back to Singapore to help my friends and I to think consciously of our lives and our actions. God bless his soul and those of many other fellow travellers who help us expand our consciousness through their own walking of the paths across space and time.

The serenity of the mountains and monasteries were a quiet call to our souls to speak up as the ever-chattering minds stood transfixed in the mystery that surrounded us. Vinod facilitated powerful conversations about sustainability, global warming, change and personal and social responsibilities. It dawned upon us the need to do our own bit to contribute to nature, to the environment and to save this planet for us, for you and for your children. Not that this was new news. There were more than enough documentaries and messages even earlier. But the Journeys with Meaning had opened doors that had gone rusty. The Journeys with Meaning introduced us to soulful hosts who had big kitchens with enough to feed their guests, big store houses that saved grains and food for the next three-seven years and bigger hearts that shared stories about conscious living, collaboration and peace on Earth. The Journeys with Meaning is a natural response by an individual to create opportunities for city dwellers to add meaning to their love for travel and to their own lives. The Journeys with Meaning is a call to truly experience one's senses of listening, seeing and feeling what we tend to numb in our every-day life. The Journeys with Meaning serves by bringing one close to nature; within and without.

The message was a visceral one coming from the depths of nature, within and without, and stayed with me even after returning to the city life. I had always perceived nature to be out there. I was reminded that nature lived within us and one of our truths was to align ourselves to the best of our own unique nature. When there is peace within, we naturally work towards peace without.

This was a reinforcing message from my quiet meditation time in Bali, from my thrilling adventurous time in the Savannahs in Africa, from my homely stays at home in the vicinity of the Himalayas, always. It was not the place one travels to alone that matters. It is getting in touch with the meaning within us that is possible even in the blink-blink of city life as long as it is practiced consciously.

My friends noticed new behaviours where I would go for long, quiet walks on my own and contemplate and be comfortable with solitude. This was an endeavour I had tried and failed many a time before. Nature makes possible what formal education and knowledge sometimes limits. My travel sojourns changed again. I sought out places to be with in nature and found aplenty both in Singapore (much to the surprise of the naysayers) and beyond.

I hope and pray for you that you enjoy your journey of life with meaning in both your inner and outer worlds. I trust you to practice seeing the same old with new eyes that will serve you and your relationships with others' true nature and nature.

Journeying with you,

Grandma

PS: So, my lovely grandchildren, what are your stories of your journeys with meaning as your *Practice of Satsang*, in your times?

"Over time, we've disconnected ourselves completely from these stories that Nature is trying to share with us. It's time to remedy that."

-Vinod Sreedhar (2014)
-(Founder at Journeys with Meaning)

Now, it is time for Practice.
You may create your own or experiment with one I suggest below.

Practice
(J)

To enjoy nature, within and without.

- Carve out solitude time from your busy schedules to go and connect with nature.
    o It could be staring at the morning, evening or night sky.
    o It could be a walk.
    o It could be meditation.
    o It could be bird-watching, bird-feeding, gardening etcetra.
- Carve out one intention into action in serving nature truthfully, in your circle of influence, within and without.

PS: Become the observer that you naturally are.

Kissing the Waves ~

~ Letters to my grandchildren ~

My dear little ones, out of the many words you will learn starting with the alphabet 'K', I have a few fundamental ones to share. In addition to 'Kite' or 'Kangaroo', words that helped me to understand the world, the outer world, I was curious to gain access to the mysterious inner world that exists within us. The secret to peace, happiness and fulfillment lies in there. Our inner world determines how we respond to the outer world - people, places and perspectives. Practicing the essence of the few fundamental words below has been life-giving, nourishing and key to expanding possibilities for me.

As you grow each day into beautiful beings, I invite you to experiment, play and discover the essence of these words in your life. As you master the game, you will get clues to master your life and create your own future that is meaningful, day-by-day. The key is to choose wisely and practice consciously. Remember, whatever you practice; consciously, sub-consciously, or unconsciously, right or wrong, it grows stronger. So, what do you choose?

K for Kaleidoscope

- What is your practice of observing your own thoughts, and others' thoughts; in relation to each other? Do they build on each other from a learning frame, or clash against each other, so the one that does not fit your frame has to be thrown away?

K for Kindergarten

- What is your school of learning and playing as you grow, in your 10s, 20s, 30s, 40s, 50s, 60s, 70s, 80s, 90s ...?
- Who are your playmates?

K for Kindness

- What is your practice to be kind to yourself and to others?

- What is your practice to accept kindness and graciousness?

Other words, still starting with 'K', also served me but only for short-term. Practice of the essence of these words fed my ego and exhausted me in the long-term as I found them to be life-depleting;

K for 'Knocked down' (and staying there), 'Knotted up' (and stuck there), and 'Karma blame' (as an excuse for not reflecting and taking action).

Practice of *Satsang* with Fellow Travellers – A Story

Kissing the Waves ~

Squeals and cries filled the air and everyone turned to look. Kicking legs, clutching arms, followed with a thunderous 'daddyyy', followed with more screams reverberating terror echoed everywhere.

Often I am witness to a similar scene where enthusiastic and patient parents bring their little ones to the edge of the sea, teaching them to enjoy the sand, waves and sun. While many toddlers are happy to get dirty, build sand castles, throw some sand at the parents, eat some sand and roll in the sand, the waves and the water element do not get the same love, at least initially. Feeling the sand slip from under their feet, the waves represent a different element in the kaleidoscope of a little child, I assume. It takes some time for the little ones to see the parents inside the water, learn to float and enjoy it too.

Bringing the metaphor to adult life, it leaves me wondering what are some adult responses to the 'sand' and the 'waves' and different elements in our lives?

Have you caught yourself on the downward sloping hill when you are longing to do some things, many things in life but for some unfathomable reason are afraid take the first step? I was happily rolling in the 'sand' and living in my own sand castle, on some roads most traveled – TV, movies, virtual world, ordering unhealthy food in because it is easier and a million other stagnant habits that ultimately did not make me happy. Even though I looked at the 'waves' longingly, like sports, travel, good reading habits etcetra, I did not dare to get my feet wet in things that I really wanted to do and found the lamest of excuses for it.

I wanted to get up and go to the waves. But the distance seemed too far.

Talking to different friends and fellow travellers, from different walks of life, the definitions of 'sand' and 'waves' changed from person to person. Some needed to speed up their lives, others needed to slow down. Both, often times, did not know how to make that switch. It gets easy to stay attached to one way of being. Getting unattached and being flexible is the switch.

Searching for that switch, I met inspiring fellow travellers, who had not only found the switch for themselves but also held the space for others to find their own unique switches too. One unique stunning fellow-traveler and friend, spread across time and space, enabled me in her own special way. Every time I met her, which might be as rare as nine times in the first five years, she seemed to be switching and playing with all elements that came along; sand, waves, gravel, stones, sea shells, sun, clouds, rains! Little wonder that not only was she able to keep the child within her alive and kicking, but the lovely lady and wise woman actually worked with many children to help reconcile with their struggles, learning curves, meaning-making of their lives!

Christy, your Singaporean Chinese grandmother, known amongst many gifts for writing children's book; Drax the Dragon, for her graphic recording skills, seemed to be playing with all the colors on the canvas converting events to wisdom, words to landscape; just as with all the colors in life, showing up as a lady, child, warrior and mid-wife.

Having completed her degree in Psychology, she dedicated herself to support her sister to open a unique kindergarten for children, using sand-play to help them express, interpret and sense – make the kaleidoscope of emotions and events in life. (*Ah! I see your wide anticipating eyes – yes, remind me to take you to meet her for sand play one of these days.*) Christy would be in the sandy gardens, sandy caves, sandy mountains, sandy families, sandy fears, sandy hopes, sandy schools and sandy tales with the little ones, listening to them, helping them find the switch, the answers, the questions.

I often wondered what kept her going, her uncanny ability to stay attuned, stay present to both children and adults and balance between adapting and creating. I realized that she loved every bit of it and practiced graciousness. She invited me to be her play-mate, in the kindergarten of life! While my mature mind tried to comprehend the meaning behind it, she had touched the heart of the child within me, who was clapping her hands in glee.

One day, out of the blue, she invited me to join her in her African drumming class. It was a group of around twenty people of varying shapes and sizes, ages, virtues and vices! There were only 2-3 of us who were novice beginners. The rest of them got together for jamming and having fun. We each got a drum and learnt the basic steps, a basic melody and were asked to play-drum along. I found myself instantaneously shrink with consternation as I concentrated to get the melody right, to play it well. My mature mind wanted to perform. The little girl in me could not keep her hands from making noise on the drum. 'How embarrassing!', my mature mind snarled. Darn!

Taddak! I hit out of tune. I focused - more.

Plap! I missed a beat. Others seemed to get it.

I turned pink. I stole a glance at her. She was drumming away! I looked at the others. I saw child-like visages smiling, in a flow, lost in their own sand castles where only they and their drums existed. Yet, magically, they could connect with each others' rhythms across the sand castles as they tuned in to play, listen and feel. It did not matter if one missed a beat or got it wrong, the idea was to just play along and trust. I looked at the teacher, who gave me an encouraging glance.

I began to play. Soft palms. Softer beats. Sometimes I got it right. Sometimes I got it wrong. The little girl in me did not stop, began to have fun and pulled out a tongue at my mature mind, who let her be. (After all this was not a competition!)

Collaboration! Rhythm! Before I knew it, my hands seemed to have a life of their own! They were in sync with all the other hands drumming in unison, drumming in joy. Heads moved with the rhythm. Smiles flashed across. We were all just one wave!

I had such fun. My real teacher in that lesson was a ten-year old child, who seemed to have the most fun. I caught him enjoy making mistakes, enjoying the music, marveling at the sound created out of his hands, unconsciously leading the group, offering a loud, re-sounding beat. I learnt the art of presence from him. He was just playing. Yet, his play turned into a compelling performance.

When does one switch from playing to performing? When does one forget to have fun to get things right? If one forgets, what a difference it makes to have a fellow traveller and friend, who is uniquely different; who experiments with unique ways of expression; whose world is a canvas open to art jamming, throwing paints on the canvas and letting the paint decide whether it wishes to stick, slip, slide, scratch or simmer with other colors. This is so different than what I had learnt in my childhood - colouring strictly between the lines!

Christy's husband, and your American grandfather, Doug, who is a guru in the field of Organisation Development, a teacher for many adult leaders and an innovator in his style of teaching, had told me of this invaluable lesson the first time I had met him. I was a novice beginner then at my work and was curious to know the secret behind dynamic facilitators and trainers, who taught and engaged adults from their hearts. I learnt it was about constant practice, play and exploration – both in one's personal and professional lives!

Coming back to the kaleidoscope of kindergarten in life, when is the last time you played a board game where winning or losing was not the criteria? In my childhood, I do not recall any game that did not end fiercely and competitively, be it with your great-great-grandparents, my parents or brother or friends! Thumb rule – always have ice-cream on the side to assuage the wounds!

One evening, Christy and Doug, invited me to play the 'Transformation Game', which they had learnt, from Findhorn Foundation, Scotland. It is a board game where one puts one's real life question on the board, throws the dice, and seeks guidance from the diverse elements on the board game and the players around. It is a collaborative game, where there is no competition as each one is on one's own journey, in search of answers to the life question one poses. The questions could be around love, life, career, growth, fears, health etc. Each player comments on the question posed by self and others. Each player listens to all the perspectives, whether one likes it or not. The game allows the players to practice to listen to and reflect upon different elements, view-points. Of course, each player chooses to take away what is most meaningful to oneself in that moment. The game allows for players to give and receive the best they can as one follows the beat of ups and downs determined by the dice!

So interesting – and different – from Ludo, Snakes and Ladder, Monopoly, Risk, Chess, Chinese Checkers or Scrabble, for example! This was unlike any other game I had ever played.

Shoe, your cool Singaporean Chinese grandmother, an epitome of love, energy and fun, a learner enthusiast was the fourth player. What a combination the four of us made! We put four hot, burning questions from each of our lives on the table and began the game. I sat back looking at my three play-mates, admiring their serene souls that could not be hidden in the game as they paid heed to each element the game brought up. Amidst laughter, tears, savory snacks, little did we realize that the board game lasted for about five hours! And nobody killed nobody!!! My first!

The fun lasted for more than five months as I tried out some ideas they had shared to walk towards the waves, without fear and with joy. Not only did I learn to swim in the waves, but I also learnt to jet ski, banana boat, ride the waves; metaphorically speaking, thanks to the wisdom of my life-long learner mates reminding me to play in life. It was a timely reminder for me when my happiness graph in life began to fall away. It was a timely test for me to get out of my comfort zone.

Christy's latest play is to consciously spend time in nature, in the gardens and parks in Singapore. She takes photographs of life in the form of birds, insects, flowers and turtles. She even creates mandalas with what nature offers (flowers and seeds) on the green grass. She shares her play through photographs which has inspired many a soul to peal themselves away from the couch and make a visit to the garden/park.

The friendship has lasted and deepened as we still meet to talk about new discoveries, new possibilities, new yearnings and new lessons.

And it all began with kindness shown in the sporadic meetings we had – some planned, some unplanned.

Keeping kindness as the intention, I scanned the horizon of my life to appreciate various fellow travellers on a sunny day on an island. Just like a picture from any beach, some like to laze around, some like to sun-bathe. Some like to play and be social, be it beach volley-ball or other, some like to be by themselves, sit and read, listen to music, and sleep. Some like to dive in, some like to stand by the shore line. Some are looking at their feet, picking up sea shells, some are leaving behind foot prints, and some are imagining the future - glued to the horizon ...

The more I sought, the more I got. All it takes is to take the first step, reach out and interact with anyone from the picture. Each fellow traveller taught me a unique lesson of life, and death! Some fellow travellers taught me to be comfortable to even converse about death. Slowly and surely, I began to have those conversations with friends first, then family too.

Another of your Singaporean Indian grandmother and my unique fellow traveller friend, Vadivu Govind, took up 'Dying before actual death' as an experiment since 2011. She is the Founder of Joy Works that creates spaces for possibilities and conversations around workplace happiness. Open to life's lessons and gifts, she has many stories to share and is a lovely storyteller. I was mesmerized like a child listening to her stories. One evening, under the full moon, we sat together by the seaside in East Coast Park, watching the waves and witnessing learning from each other's life-experiments. What really struck me the most was her 'death experiments', where she imagined her death on December 31, in the January of the same year. Starting January 1, she began to live a life of consciousness and awareness, epitomizing living each day as if it were her last! Developing a powerful practice of reflection as this, as to how might she live her life, knowing that she would die on a given date, she observed herself on how the experiment made an impact.

In her own words, "Since I can die at anytime and would have things undone, I need to find peace with how I have traveled and not be overly destination-focused. I need to find peace with how I have treated people on the way and whether I was present to their needs; whether I have learned from them; how I have picked myself up when I have fallen; whether I could give and receive in greater balance; whether I knew when to speed up and when to slow down and when to stop and rest; whether I enjoyed the scenery; whether I looked where I was going; whether I knew which signs to follow; whether I knew when to take an unexpected path; and whether I was clear that the destination I wanted to go towards demanded of me - love, wisdom, truth, growth, service and joy."

"It has helped me say "yes" to things I wouldn't have without this experiment. These are things that have demanded much courage and effort from me but which were very important for the welfare of others. I feel more liberated from fears and inhibitions.

It has helped me value relationships more.

It has helped me love more deeply and expansively, even if it is difficult.

It has helped me figure out what I need to act urgently on.

It has helped me cherish my family more.

It helped me give my dog a better life and death.

It has helped me think more about whether I'm living a balanced life."

The practice of 'dying before actual death' became the wind beneath Joy Works' wings and an inspirational fellow traveller's tale for the rest of us.

Just like it is difficult to distinguish the waters from the various rivers that make the sea, it is difficult to distinguish the richness in life-lessons I have received from diverse fellow travellers, who create practices in their own lives to stay agile, alert and accomplished. Not only that, they also share with abundant kindness so we may co-create a better world for you. We are trying.

I hope and pray for you that you cultivate the courage to kiss the waves of life bravely. I trust you to practice kindness in your inner world for yourself and in your relationships.

Kissing you,

Grandma

PS: So, my lovely grandchildren, what are your stories of kindness and games that you play nobly as your *Practice of Satsang*, in your times?

"BE so attractive inside and out that the other has no choice."

-Christy Lee-O' Loughlin (2013)
(Graphic Recorder, Soul Gardener)

Now, it is time for Practice.
You may create your own or experiment with one I suggest below.

Practice
(K)

To practice accepting diverse shades of yourself both when you were in your comfort zone and out of your comfort zone. A question that has often guided well is, 'When is the last time you did something for the first time?' Some people answer that with a reticent 'Why do you have to do new things in the first place?' Sit with both these questions and discover your own truth for yourself.

- Think of a time when you were at your best. You were someone people looked up to, admired and you were in flow doing what you loved. What were your strengths that you cultivated and practiced to be at that high?
- Think of a time when you are at your lowest point in life. Everything that mattered to you was falling apart. What made you persevere and continue despite the tears, fears and extreme challenges?
- Think of a time when you were bored out of your mind. Everyone and everything seemed static around you. What confluence of thoughts and emotions pushed/pulled you to change the situation?
- Think of a time when you displayed wisdom as an adult in your childhood days. Think of a time when you displayed child like freshness in your adulthood days.

PS: Honour and keep alive the diverse shades in yourself that makes the best of who you are.

The Lullaby of Love ~

~ Letters to my grandchildren ~

My dear little ones, out of the many words you will learn starting with the alphabet 'L', I have a few fundamental ones to share. In addition to 'Lion' or 'London', words that helped me to understand the world, the outer world, I was curious to gain access to the mysterious inner world that exists within us. The secret to peace, happiness and fulfillment lies in there. Our inner world determines how we respond to the outer world - people, places and perspectives. Practicing the essence of the few fundamental words below has been life-giving, nourishing and key to expanding possibilities for me.

As you grow each day into beautiful beings, I invite you to experiment, play and discover the essence of these words in your life. As you master the game, you will get clues to master your life and create your own future that is meaningful, day-by-day. The key is to choose wisely and practice consciously. Remember, whatever you practice; consciously, sub-consciously, or unconsciously, right or wrong, it grows stronger. So, what do you choose?

L for Love

- What does love mean to you? What does love mean to the person you choose to love?
- Who are you as a person, who are you becoming as a person, when you accept that you *are* love and that love is not what another person brings to you?

L for Life-giving

- What is life-nurturing, life-nourishing, life-giving for you?
- Who expands your love for life, both when you are up and when you are down? For whom do you care deeply in the same way?

L for Loyalty

- What are the non-negotiables in your life that you stand by?

- What do you do to respect yours and others' non-negotiables, irrespective of whether they match yours or not?

Other words, still starting with 'L', also served me but only for short-term. Practice of the essence of these words fed my ego and exhausted me in the long-term as I found them to be life-depleting;

L for 'Lethargic', 'Lamentable' and 'Lustful'.

Practice of *Satsang* with Fellow Travellers – A Story

The Lullaby of Love ~

When I was three years old, I was told that my love of my life and prince charming will come on a horse and ride with me into the sun set for a happily ever after life. I saw photos of happy people on horseback in Darjeeling with the snow-peaked mountains in the distance and I believed.

When I was thirteen years old, I had fallen in love! Eureka!!! Only it had happened more than once, unlike in the fairy tales! Uh Oh! Whatever had happened to the 'happily ever after' the very first time? My first time was a complete disaster. Family and even friends had the audacity to call my 'true love' a teenage crush (of course it was in the teenage years. But at that age, *that* love is true, oh so true!) Why is the fairy tale and Bollywood characters' love at first sight called love and the same kind of love in real life called a crush?

When I was twenty - three years old, I had read other books like Mills & Boon to confirm my belief in fairy tales. I was waiting for my tall-dark-and-handsome despite the Indian advertisements furiously promoting Fairness creams for even the men, and of course women (the latter goes without saying!). I should have sniffed out something was not quite right then but starry-eyed, I was waiting for my turn to fall in love. Bollywood movies meanwhile reinforced the message with soul-wrenching music, dance and stories.

I was thoroughly confused about love and found out from other girl and guy friends in college that so were they. Once bitten twice shy! We would listen to a kaleidoscope of stories of love, romance, lust, break-ups, bizarre chasings, loyalty, marriage, sex and sexuality. We wanted to be well informed and real informed to make our choices.

It is worth noticing what are the stories that abound in our culture on all these topics? Also, it is important to observe the conversations that occur and more importantly, those that do not occur. Notice the absence or presence of teaching the young ones the skills of inquiry and reflection around the same topics with their peers, friends, fellow travellers and loves of their lives. Jokes, real-life stories and things that are taboo are also rich sources of information for any given culture. Except that the information is twisted and turned in some forms.

There was a time when I launched a 'Love project' with some friends. The purpose was to find out more about Love. So, we spoke to the singles and the married couples and the estranged ones. It left us amused, shocked, bewildered, confused and also strangely, loved! There is an instant connection as people love to talk about love.

"Erm…love…wait, let me think!' – followed with maniacal laughter or deep silence or a string of hurried and stuttered words were the most oft response.

"Love is errrrrrrrrrr…………"

"Love is friendship. I want to be friends with the one I love and marry."

"Love is happiness. It makes you happy. You make the one you love happy."

"Love is watching the sun-rise, sun-set, stars, eating peanut butter, ice-cream, dancing, singing, painting, spreading happiness and joy."

"I want to get married and fall in love because everyone is doing so."

"Love is that divine feeling that feels good."

"Love happens naturally after marriage."

"Love to me is pure, loving my family, caring for them, ensuring that they are safe, good, and happy. That makes me happy."

"I am lonely. I want love."

"Love is what you make it out to be."

"I like the idea of falling in love."

"Love is a game of hormones."

"Love is an emotion that encompasses different emotions! The word love is over-used in our times. The Greeks had it right; where romantic love, sexual love, love for family and community and God was described distinctly."

"Love is respect. Love is trust. Love is passion."

"I believe love is expansive, for the whole of humankind. If only we could see how we are all connected, we are all one and learn to love everyone."

"Love is doing my work, performing my duties in the best way."

Every person has a unique definition-in-progress of love, definitely a personal experience that sometimes cannot be described in words and a personal history with an aspiration for the future.

What is Love for you?

Talking about love has the potential to be one of the best universal icebreakers, accompanied of course with the sensitive question, depending with whom you are talking to, and in which context. 'How did you meet uncle/aunty, Mr.../Mrs...?' to an aged couple opens up the streams of memories and the stories begin to pour out. 'How did you discover your passion about this?' to a committed artist, researcher, student or professional unlocks the romance with one's own work/art. 'Do you have a boyfriend/girlfriend?' to a young child brings forth a blush and tales from the school, if not from the child, from the friends/family!!!

What I learnt from that project was how some people responded about love from a place of love. And it was not just love between the sexes or even between the same sex. Some people who responded lovingly about love had a calmness about them that was very attractive. They had shining soft eyes, sometimes even with deep lines and a beautiful smile. They were truly an embodiment of love itself. Some were with their partners, some were even without. The latter category got us curious and we found out that they were truly in love with a special passion/art/hobby that mattered to them and gave meaning to their life.

What?!! Love is not about the prince charming ... and the horse ... and the sunset! Oh no! I was baffled, completely.

Alternatively, there were others who responded about love from a place of fear, from a place of losing love. That was not attractive.

Ah yes! I had heard many stories of the latter.

Somewhere, it began to dawn upon us that perhaps love is truly an internal state than an external person.

S i l e n c e.

Perhaps love is a state of being that is possible to be irrespective of whether you are with that special someone or not.

M o r e   s i l e n c e.

And a silent truth, "But I want to be with that special someone."

Our human species cannot escape love!

Our human species, for centuries, has men and women struggling with questions around love. Our human species nurtures stories of love from generation to generation, despite war, famine, destruction, richness, life and death!!!

What if we pause to look and re-look at those stories?

I did so. I had witnessed many a heart-break, mine own and that of other friends too. When one happens, friends and fellow travellers instantly empathise. Many offer to listen. Many offer to 'bitch'. Many offer to drown the heart-ache in various innovative ways. But what one really looks for is love and healing.

I read, listened and learnt. Bear with me and this lullaby as I sing to you my favourite numbers and self-written lyrics!

Among zillions of definitions on love, my favourite is to quote Humbarto Maturana, Chilean biologist and philosopher.

Love is the only emotion that expands intelligence.

Irrespective of how one describes love in language, akin to prayer and meditation, that feeling, I believe, is exquisite, where a person with loving eyes sees the world differently. Other life-energizing attributes as laughter, gratitude, generosity, forgiveness, inspiration, meaning comes easier to a person with love in one's heart – irrespective of the situation one is in.

Yet, it is a paradox as it is so difficult and yet, so easy to be open in love, to have a loving heart and an awake consciousness to respond to everything with love. After all if energy only expands and contracts, and is not born and does not die, then it is a matter of noticing your own energy each day and that of another person, even if it is a loved one, a situation or a place.

Next, it is a matter of choice to respond with love versus in a reactive manner and see the difference that makes. All kinds of energy surrenders to the energy of love as that is the most expansive of all energies. It reminded me of Physics lessons when I first heard of it. As I began to practice it bit by bit, the beauty of this began to unfold. So, for example, I experimented and chose to respond to an emotion of fear or anger or jealousy or hatred with love. The situation could be defined in many ways. The person may be a family member, a friend, a loved one or one whom you like. The story could be anything but learning to let go of it all and to just let in love was enough. It changed people, their perspectives, my perspective and our relationships.

This change may take time, as people are sometimes surprised and even shocked when you respond with love. It becomes important to take care of yourself and your energy as you are practising to respond differently. Walk away from the energy vampires and the psychic trolls disguised in love!

There was this phase when everyone asked me if I were in love as I was so zen-like and happy, truly happy, practising this experiment. I realized I was in love – with the energy of love, which was not restricted to one person and not dependent on an external person. It emanated from within. I felt the expansion and my love for humanity and even for pets; dogs and cats. I have always been afraid of animals. It was a new sensation to see and experience compassion, to experience love and fulfillment. It felt like the unconditional love of a mother, though I have no experience yet of what that truly is. It felt like the unconditional love of nature, of the universe. I had finally risen in love!

I learnt that the stories I had heard since I was a child focused on the love between a man and a woman, primarily. But do you have sleepless nights if you do find the right person, at the right time, as has been decided right by others?

I also learnt that many people force themselves to be in love for fear of being alone. This fear is fired by culture too. In my culture, arranged marriage is the norm. I have heard innumerable questions from people of other cultures trying to understand this norm. I have heard innumerable answers from people of my culture who explain the origins, benefits or fall-outs of this norm.

I have just been in honest contemplation of when, how and if this norm fits to the truth of who I am, with no judgment for others' truths.

Often times I have heard my well-wishers ask me to get married before it is "too late". Except when I was eighteen, twenty-three was considered too late. When I turned twenty-three, twenty-five became too late. I have not reached my thirties. I am in the too late phase. I am finally free as I realize for me, "Love is freedom and marriage is celebrating the truth of that love".

Love and Freedom. What is your definition of that?

I realized my truth long time ago as a child but forgot and remembered again and forgot again. There were times when I believed in the truth of "too late" and was rushing against time. There was this phase when all my friends were getting married and I was swiftly finding myself to be the only single attending events attended to by couples. It was unnerving and I had reached the tip of desperation to be with someone, anyone, just so that I would not be by myself. The harder I tried, the more difficult it was to find anyone. One day, I was very agitated as another wedding event was drawing close. Close to tears, I put on my running shoes to get some fresh air and went for a run. I was running against everything. I was sprinting. My lungs were bursting. I wished the universe would swallow me as it was so difficult to live with my truth. Wait, what is my truth?

Hours after, as the air cooled my wounded and wound nerves, as the ground threw me up in the air ever so lightly like an adult throws a little baby in the air and catches back to the giggles and delight of the baby, I suddenly stopped short in my tracks. I suddenly 'saw' my own insanity. I began laughing. I had been searching for love and others had been searching for me my right one to be married to. Both perspectives were correct but with all the pressure, it seemed as if the perspectives were like parallel running lines of a train track!

I was fighting against receiving love in my search for love. I was afraid to give love and be open to it. I expected another to love me when I could not bring myself to love me. I expected another to spend time with me when I could not bring myself to be in my own company. Every person I met, I distanced myself with. Yet, deep within, I wanted connection. I was in search of love out of fear! Little wonder, that if my energy was contracting, getting smaller and smaller, how could I recognize the expansive energy of love? Even if I saw it, I was so afraid of it for losing myself in it. I had to find love but not outside, in the dating events or on the websites.

I choose to find love by being love.

I returned home, relieved and happy, and physically exhausted. The search was worth it. I had found my truth. Many things that I had read in books and seen in movies had not prepared me for that phase. Yet, quietening the inner turmoil of emotions of fear that has a snowball effect was a switch button. And just like that I was out of that phase! I decided to concentrate on my feelings and my inner truth than the reality painted and advocated by the external world of 'musts' and 'shoulds'. I attended the wedding, not comparing myself with her or this and that but just radiating love, comfortable to be the only single in a group of lovely coupled up friends.

My friends celebrated my truth with me. Some friends exacerbated that fear for they themselves are fearful. Some are in a different place. Choose your peer pressure. Recognize the difference and help yourself and others. I basked in the love of those friends whose well-meaning advice of self-care I had been ignoring. No more!

After that I chose to be alone for a while and take up that time to be one of discovery, exploration, unlearning and living. Solitude is a great opportunity to reflect, to be, to do what you have always wished to but have never had the time to do so. Alone is different from lonely and one can be lonely even when one is with one's life partner. Also, life and death have their own truth and one can find oneself with or without a partner. How can we still celebrate love?

Self-Love! I had never heard of that. Infact, I had heard of narcissistic love, selfish love, but not self-love. Life had given me enough evidence to show that one who does not respect oneself, one who is not at peace with oneself, one who does not have practices to be in joyful solitude with oneself, one who is in constant search for someone else to love her/him, carries that dissatisfaction even in the relationship.

Loving out of self-love is a state of loving and honouring yourself, knowing that you are a work-in-progress; forgiving yourself, giving your best, failing, trying again and believing that you can love and be loved. I experienced this state of being when I felt accomplished just knowing that I was learning as a student (even if I did not get straight A's), when I had a sense of identity as a teenager (even if others made fun of my identity but I did not give in to peer pressure), when I had a sense of purpose as a young person (even if others did not see it), when I had a job (even if others did not want me to have one), when I had fun with meaningful experiments in life! I realized that in that state I was a kind, compassionate, brave, strong woman for whom love meant to grow.

Self-love helped me to be selfless as I helped the other person grow too. Similarly, it helped me be open to allow the other person to help me grow too.

Loving out of fear is a state of self-doubt, plagued with self-limiting thoughts, guilt, anger, extreme sense of justice, frustration, jealousy, trying to love as prescribed by the outside world - religion, culture, norms, trends, but not truly believing in it. I experienced this state of being so many times in my life, when I compared myself with other students, tried to fit in as a teenager, had a sense of competition and ego as a young person, wanted the other person to change, or went on a self-depreciating parade of a string of compromises made, where I was really just feeding that monster of anger or guilt in the guise of love. There was practically no space for love as other strong emotions took up the space in my relationship with others, with work, with life. I realized that in that state I was a weak, afraid woman for whom love became a struggle, a display of ego and a terrible show!

Selfish love left me depleted, even more than before.

Honest inquiry, a conversation with a loved one and an admission when one feels fear instead of love is enough to be aware and to reset one's button back to love. Few amazing questions that I have collected from various fellow travellers and that have evolved and guided me over and over again have been:

- "What is your relationship with yourself?" or "Are you attuned to taking care of yourself; nourishing yourself regularly - physically, emotionally, and spiritually?"
- "What practices support you in being with yourself, in calm and confident solitude, as with others, in connection?"
- "Are you willing to be vulnerable and honest and allow another to be so?"

I hope and pray that you arise in love and sing the lullaby of love that is life giving for you and your loved one. I trust you to practice ways of self-love and remain loyal to love, out of love and not fear.

Singing a lullaby for you, and LOVING you,

Grandma

PS: So, my lovely grandchildren, what are your love stories as your *Practice of Satsang,* in your times?

"Be in a relationship because you have found someone whom you love and who allows you to be yourself fully and completely. Love and Freedom go together. Enjoy it. The freedom to choose intimacy, the freedom to love unconditionally and the freedom to be the full expression of who you are and who we are meant to be with another."

-Diana Jean Reyes (2014)
-(Soul Sister & Friend,

Career Coach & Facilitator
from Philippines in Singapore)

"You have to put your heart out there. It is a risk knowing that you will experience pain and joy, and pain and joy again. Do not get attached to any one state of being. Do not get stuck. You have full control/choice over one thing – your state of being. Be free."

-Chris Balsley (2013)
-(Owner, Landonwerks Inc,
Newfield Network LLC,

Tension-Release Exercises Teacher & Coach
Paraphrasing above quote that helped me get unstuck)

Now, it is time for Practice.
You may create your own or experiment with one I suggest below.

Practice
(L)

To practice self love that is life giving for others and helping others practice too.

- Schedule self-love or 'me' time every day, even if it is for five minutes! Protect that time from your loved one, your children, your family and

friends. Do nothing or do something that is nourishing for you in that
time. Be Free.

- Dance!
  Allow your body to move the way it wishes too and connect with yourself,
  your breath, your rhythm.

PS: Tell yourself and your loved ones that you love them, often.

PART
4

Practice of *Satsang* with Colleagues, Clients

Mimicking is not Mastery ~

~ Letters to my grandchildren ~

My dear little ones, out of the many words you will learn starting with the alphabet 'M', I have a few fundamental ones to share. In addition to 'Money' or 'Monkey', words that helped me to understand the world, the outer world, I was curious to gain access to the mysterious inner world that exists within us. The secret to peace, happiness and fulfillment lies in there. Our inner world determines how we respond to the outer world - people, places and perspectives. Practicing the essence of the few fundamental words below has been life-giving, nourishing and key to expanding possibilities for me

As you grow each day into beautiful beings, I invite you to experiment, play and discover the essence of these words in your life. As you master the game, you will get clues to master your life and create your own future that is meaningful, day-by-day. The key is to choose wisely and practice consciously. Remember, whatever you practice; consciously, sub-consciously, or unconsciously, right or wrong, it grows stronger. So, what do you choose?

M for Mindfulness; even about Money; while Mailing; in Meetings!

- When have you recognized mindfulness, especially at workplaces?
- When have you been mindful, especially at workplaces?

M for Motivation

- What is motivating for you?
- What is your understanding of what motivates others?

M for Mystery and Miracles

- What are the mysteries you unravel, especially at workplaces?
- What miracles are you grateful for, especially at workplaces?

Other words, still starting with 'M', also served me but only for short-term. Practice of the essence of these words fed my ego and exhausted me in the long-term as I found them to be life-depleting;

M for 'Misconduct', 'Misery' and 'Morbidity'.

Practice of *Satsang* with Colleagues, Clients – A Story

Mimicking is not Mastery ~

'Is Practice of *Satsang* even possible with colleagues and clients in organisations? Family, Friends and Fellow travellers, I can understand but in the world structured with competition, greed, apathy, inhumanity, making money as the prime motive, is it possible to have higher ideals and practices that truly matter?', an exasperated friend asked, after a long day, month, year at work, questioning the dignity of human beings.

I held the question posed in silence.

I do not know.

Actually, a part of me does know, it is possible because I have experienced it over and over again. In competitive workplaces, even with structures of bonuses and best employee statuses, I have seen colleagues use collaborative practices and remain ethical. It is not that I am 'just lucky'. Or, is it? I wonder. I have found myself looking out for it, and have invariably seen it. Once the act of kindness, generosity, hard work and heart work, even with colleagues, is acknowledged, it gets reinforced and practiced naturally.

Like any other practice, and with family, friends or fellow travellers, one has to work for it to build relationship with colleagues and clients. All it needs is a motive that is meaningful to you.

I am very grateful though that I was blessed with leaders in organisations who were not only role models, but also great teachers. I have had my share of good and bad leaders and colleagues. I have learnt an invaluable lesson from each of them. The good ones fill you up with inspiration that enhances your work and motivates your core to emulate them. The other ones also have the capability to call upon dormant strengths in you that make you stand up for your beliefs, work and values. Also, you now know what you do not want to become, when you get in that position.

This core of who we are as persons can never be restricted only to our personal lives and switched off from nine to five! If anything, it is the most challenging and important hours to practice so that we are not living a disparate life because we cannot split the core of who we are into two halves! We can choose to be someone who spends ball park of one's energy resisting to go to work, then preparing to go to work, then working, then jumping out of it as if it were the plague, or complaining because she/he has to take work back home and cannot say no to the boss. We can choose to be someone who explores what is her/his indicator of success, finds the kind of work that aligns with the personal indicators, finds meaning at work and attempts to build conscious professional relations at work. The latter is not impossible. As a practitioner, you can choose to practice mindfulness, resilience and compassion, or mindlessness, greed and intentional competition to harm others, irrespective of the workplace's policies. Sure, one always has valid reasons for one's choices. Is it out of fear, or out of care that you choose what you choose, at workplaces?

Practice does make us perfect, but the question is what are we practicing?

I have seen many leaders, who use fear and power or authority for their brand of leadership. They split people at work for their own gains. Many such leaders spend their time, potential and energy in fire-fighting drills. They end up with recalcitrant followers, who rarely contribute, do not care and resign. Little do the leaders realize that they are causing a catastrophe not only for themselves and others at the workplace, but that the stress trickles down to hundreds and thousands of families when angry, stressed, de-motivated people return home, dissatisfied with the dynamics at work.

On the other hand, I have also seen many leaders and colleagues work with their teams about their personal and collective/organisational identities and vision. They focus on the people. They focus on what their people are truly capable of. They call on their people to tackle a crisis, affirm their learning and growth, and support them to take risks to challenge their own weaknesses. The strategies, tactics, technology are structures to enable the people to perform. This leads to trust where people are willing to go the extra mile, are motivated to contribute, care and create. They go home, ready to rest and have some resonant time with their loved ones.

I was blessed to have an ideal, inspiring leader in the first job I ever stuck around for a bit. It has been a well-known woe of our generation for the Human Resources that unlike our parents' generation, we do not necessarily stick to one job for years. I recall your great-grandfather's shock when he heard that I had switched two jobs in less than six months. He has always inspired me and reminded me of values that I have tried my best to integrate. He believes in sticking to one job for a longer period of time to truly learn and comprehend the nature of the business, its people and its cycles. He also let me make my choices when I shared that I needed to experiment. He helped me gain clarity on what my experimentation was in service of. I was looking for an ideal job that upheld a meaningful cause that would serve humanity.

I did get one. It was in 'the real world' of the financial city and hub of India, Mumbai. I was committed to the cause of spreading awareness, and hence prevention of HIV/AIDS and its impact in both education institutions, in industries and in the corporate. There was a societal and a business case to it. It included modules to spread awareness about media influence on beauty, on our lives and our choices. It included modules to empower adolescents with life skills. It included modules to engage adults in dialogue to reflect and to contribute. It included a call to stop discrimination against people suffering from the fatal disease. It was a choice I had made between two job offers; spreading awareness for cancer or for HIV/AIDS. Both had resources, opportunities, empowering people to work with. I chose the latter because at that time, it felt it was more challenging. Unlike cancer, HIV/AIDS was/is stigmatized and therefore needs more resilience and passion to bring about mental shifts. I decided it was a great learning opportunity to immerse myself in practices to suspend judgment, question, and bring about a shift in one's perception about lifestyles, choices and people.

My first day for my new job:

I woke up early. I felt pride in the cause and the journey I was about to embark on. It was a dream come true to get a job after my education of my liking. I wanted to give my best. I showered, had some breakfast and was ready to leave for work. Almost imperceptibly, I found myself pulling up my armour suit. I felt a need to hide my happy emotions. I had always heard of dissecting the personal from professional life.

I wondered, when in our culture does one learn to consciously or sub-consciously, pull up the warrior front when it comes to work? Why do people do it - to be ready for attack or defense?

I met my colleagues. I did not get the warrior sense from any of them. They were, if anything, warm and welcoming. Could I trust what I saw and felt? It was a small team headed by Richa, who was the head in the Mumbai branch. I got to know the team bit by bit. Sitting for lunch together, listening to their conversation, one could not miss the pride in their voices as they spoke about the work they had done in the field, the new ideas they had to implement and how grateful they were for new people to join in on their team. The little nagging voice in my head kept looking for a snag. It could not be so ideal, after all.

My first week in my new job:

I was to accompany Richa with another colleague to a school where I was to observe how the workshops take place. They had worked hard for it, ensuring everything was in place. Despite that, a game that would help bring home important teaching points went amiss from the resources we had carried to the school that was important in the workshop. Within the next few minutes, I observed them brainstorming on innovative ways to create a game without the resource that would meet the same objective. There was conflict in the brainstorming but something akin to a healthy tension, where the focus was not on the persons involved but on what would serve the school. I heartily joined the discussion. If two is a crowd, three was a roar and I ended my first week on a high note of learning, connecting, observing and discerning of the small things that make a difference. In the upcoming weeks, one thing remained constant. We always struggled to make things better and to implement the Gestalt of all ideas.

I always had my observation hat on. Each of my colleagues had a beautiful balance of work-life ratio, and they respected that of each other. Their lives were not necessarily divided into personal or professional halves, but integrated in a wholistic way that allowed them to work passionately, and properly. Richa's world centered on her then, two years old daughter. She would call her every day, once, during lunch hour to check in if she were ok. I would see her dedicate similar care and understanding, to the children in the schools, especially the difficult ones. The rest of us had a chant that when we would become mothers, we would mimic Richa, an amazing leader at work!

My first year in the new job:

Simple events remain etched in the memory for a lifetime. Speaking of work-life ratio, another of my collegue, Shailesh Vaite was avidly practising some Buddhist meditation practices those days. One day, I was supposed to meet him for a programme in a couple of hours. He urgently messaged Richa, keeping me in cc, expressing that it would take all his will to be mentally present that day at work. He explained that his soul would go to the talk, about which he had read in that morning newspaper, which His Holiness, the Dalai Lama XIV, would be giving in Mumbai. I jumped to get my newspaper. Instead of helping, I cried out that it would be impossible for me to be present too with this new news. I had just returned from Mcleodganj, where His Holiness stays, but had missed him there too.

Richa messaged us simply – 'Both of you owe me for going for this talk and informing me last minute. I will attend to this programme today, do not worry.'

Later on in life, I realized that her response was golden! Leaders do not empathise to that extent generally. She could do that because she knew her team's inner worlds.

Shamelessly, Shailesh and I went for the talk. It was a one-time life opportunity. Gratefully, we excelled in everything we did thereafter at work. Most importantly, till this date, every time I smile at the thought of being in the presence of His Holiness that one time, I say a silent 'thank you' to Richa's holy generosity. She was a leader who taught us to go the extra mile even for your colleagues. She treated us as if we were her clients too.

She had her ups and downs too, all too visible to us. She would rant and take out her frustrations in the safe space we had co-created as a team. Our field of work was a challenging one. It was sensitive work too. Despite the difficulties, and in spite of her own ranting, she would always look for something positive to go by. She had much influence on both internal and external stakeholders, simply because she truly listened to them. She would have lunch with us and request us to make use of that time as the safe space where we could speak our minds, hopes and frustrations from both personal and professional lives. We could also share that which should not/must not be spoken of, as career change, pros and cons of resigning. We would share our honest thoughts with each other. But the ground rule was clear – if we choose to resign, we might as well do that. If we were there, we might as well work well. Nothing short of commitment and the best was expected.

The safe space was not only for sharing but also for strengthening. We would give and receive support and feedback on improving our technique, ideas and implementation plans. The safe space allowed us to share our successes and celebrate on a regular basis. The safe space gave a chance to share one's dreams. That is how I shared my dream of journalism and experimented with writing for the first time; from proposals and reports to articles that were even sent to the local newspapers, much to my delight.

With the passage of time, I forgot about my invisible armour suit that had gathered dust in the invisible closet, until one day, new news rushed in.

Richa resigned to move to Italy with her husband. New Delhi office was to preside over as Head in the interim. Our team was sad as we saw the writing on the wall. Soon, one by one, many people left. One was going to get married. Another one finally decided to pursue studies. So on and so forth. Many of my colleagues resigned. I still loved my job, the cause and had grown in my skills to do programmes by myself. The potential for me to step up sprung alive. I decided to stay.

I realized there was a lot at stake, communicating with the larger system and stakeholders in our Head Office, New Delhi. Tempted to put up my armour suit, feeling insecure, I mimicked Richa and what I had learnt from her. It worked, somewhat.

After a while, for months, the Mumbai team was reduced to two ladies, just Suvarna Gore and me. That did not faze us and the work results graph was still on the rise. We did need help, especially with the industrial sector, where it was important to have a male colleague. We wrote to the Head office seeking support. One of our male colleagues was sent down. To this day, I cannot fathom if it were the dynamics of 'Delhi' meeting 'Mumbai', although both of us were neither from Delhi nor Mumbai or if it were the dynamics of my ego playing up as the one in charge, or if it were just pure intentions that went awry as mistakes happened and authentic conversations did not happen. Before I knew it, I had my armour suit, shining and glinting, thirsty for blood, on! I could not mimic any longer. After a painful period of working together, where the two of us could not see each other eye-to-eye, he left.

Months later, after hard work and perseverance, Suvarna and I were very excited to travel up North to Delhi and then to beautiful Nainital with the entire office for our annual retreat. Looking at the snow clad mountain tops, beautiful tucked away resort, overlooking the greens that had a white blanket over it, we all stood mesmerized. Even in that picturesque view, nothing could assuage the hostility I felt for my 'enemy'. The armour suit became a part of me.

Eating fresh apples and apricots after a blessed dinner by the fireside, people began to retire. Suvarna and I wanted to hang out with our new-found Delhi friends. We went out for a walk together. The crisp, clear, quiet, mountain air carried a voice over to our side from afar. It was the 'enemy's' voice! He was talking to someone, another colleague presumably, his friend!

I froze!

He was bad-mouthing about me. I was embarrassed. I was angry. I was shocked. I wanted to confront him but one of my new-found friends stopped me and put things in perspective. He shared that it was because my 'enemy' had felt hurt, alone and lost in Mumbai. He was not proud of his work in Mumbai and was doubtful of his capabilities. I was numb. 'It still does not justify the things he bad-mouthed about me, which is not even true', a small voice piped up in my head. 'The others know that too and that is why they befriended you and shared with you something more significant than what you heard accidently', a stronger but quieter voice whispered, in my heart.

The last thing I wanted to do was to hurt a person's self esteem and trust in one's own capabilities. After the entire struggle in my life where I had hoped others would trust me and my dream of making a positive difference by having an education and a job, the last thing I wanted was to be the reason of a shattered hope and broken dream of another. If it mattered in our job to build the esteem of every child in school and help expand the consciousness of every person in the industrial/corporate world, how could I pretend that my 'enemy' and colleague and his self-esteem did not matter?

I ran back to my room and could not sleep that night, sobbing away into the pillow, listening to the hollow voice of my ego batter louder than the howling cold winter winds outside. I had called my colleague 'my enemy'. I had heard him bad-mouthing me but that was because of the bad experiences I had created when he was in Mumbai. I had wanted to be liked and respected for my work. I had failed. I had failed Richa. I had failed my education and my parents. When everything was dark, but not as dark as my inner world, and the self-gratifying sobs subsided, I turned in the darkness to look at my own darkness.

Who was I? Who was I becoming? Who did I wish to become?

What was important in that situation?

I had a choice to take responsibility even if it felt cold like the snow outside or be a coward and disappear like the mist in the mountains.

Instead of building strengths and a safe space, the invaluable lessons I had learnt from Richa and my old team, I had built a war zone when my colleague had come to Mumbai. I was proud of the spoils of our war in Mumbai. I had engaged his weaknesses than engaging his dreams or strengths. I did not have the learning lens when he came to Mumbai but chose to have competitive lens. What mattered was not him, nor his status of 'enemy' or 'friend', but would I be my own enemy or friend? What mattered was not that he respects me, or others respect me, but could I respect myself? Why was I doing this job? What was my vision?

What lay under the surface, were questions to look at my core beliefs of what did I want to achieve, what did I truly care about and what did I let come in the way?

Mimicking was not good enough. As a trainer of life skills, I had to discipline myself first, honestly looking at my perceptions and beliefs, before I could demand that of others. Discrimination takes places in myriad ways and if I were the perpetrator, I had to question my motives and mental models.

It was my first ever break down in work life. It was for good measure.

The next day the sun peeped out of the mist and the clouds in the mountains. I had a long way to go on the path of personal mastery. I did not have the courage then to face my 'enemy'. So I focused on my friends, meaning in my work and vowed to learn to create safe spaces that bring the best out of other people, clients or colleagues.

Fast forward, the relations and actions we sow, is what we reap. I am glad to harvest abundance on the path of mastery, where I meet old and new colleagues. I hope and pray for you that you discern between mimicking and mastering in your inner world and in your professional relationships. I trust you to practice mindfulness at work.

Mind you, look beyond the surface!

Mothering you,

Grandma

PS: So, my lovely grandchildren, what are your stories of motivating and accessing mysteries and miracles even at workplaces as your *Practice of Satsang*, in your times?

"We tried to be honest towards the contribution we were making in the field of our work. We supported and encouraged each other, brought in new ideas and worked from our heart. I guess that was somewhere the key to our happiness at work. Not to forget, we were emotionally sensitive to each other's life situations. ."

-Richa Lal (2014)
(A Leader with a difference)

"No good comes out of getting angry, worry or competition. The only thing from which any good comes out is happiness. So ensure happiness within and around."

-Shailesh Vaite (2014)
(International Social Development Consultant)

Now, it is time for Practice.
You may create your own or experiment with one I suggest below.

Practice
(M)

To be mindful. To develop mastery.

- Read up on mindfulness or meditation practices and see which one speaks to you to be true to yourself in both personal and professional life.
- Choose a practice that helps you to be aware of your emotions, your body, what is happening at the moment as an hourly chime so that you can access your whole intelligence to respond to situations at work or other.
- Get to know your strengths and weaknesses, light and shadow sides so that you can mindfully engage the best in you. Get to know that center of peace and calm in you which is stillness, peace and love.

P.S. Breathe and become friends with your breath to inform you of opportunities and costs.

Nets & Nettles Nest ~

~ Letters to my grandchildren ~

My dear little ones, out of the many words you will learn starting with the alphabet 'N', I have a few fundamental ones to share. In addition to 'Numbers' or 'Night', words that helped me to understand the world, the outer world, I was curious to gain access to the mysterious inner world that exists within us. The secret to peace, happiness and fulfillment lies in there. Our inner world determines how we respond to the outer world - people, places and perspectives. Practicing the essence of the few fundamental words below has been life-giving, nourishing and key to expanding possibilities for me

As you grow each day into beautiful beings, I invite you to experiment, play and discover the essence of these words in your life. As you master the game, you will get clues to master your life and create your own future that is meaningful, day-by-day. The key is to choose wisely and practice consciously. Remember, whatever you practice; consciously, sub-consciously, or unconsciously, right or wrong, it grows stronger. So, what do you choose?

N for Nurturing

- Who has nurtured your skills, your strengths, your hopes, especially at workplaces?
- What are you spending your time and energy in nurturing in workplaces? Who and what is benefitting from what you are nurturing?

N for Nimbleness

- What nimbleness in thoughts, words and actions allows for teams to work through things, work together, to create what matters?
- What is your nimbleness in thoughts, words and actions to sustain yourself?

N for Nature and Natural

- What decisions and choices are natural for growth, for individual and the whole?
- What decisions and choices take nature into consideration? What is your role to make this a natural way of thinking?

Other words, still starting with 'N', also served me but only for short-term. Practice of the essence of these words fed my ego and exhausted me in the long-term as I found them to be life-depleting;

N for 'Narcissism', 'Neediness' and 'Nihilism'

Practice of *Satsang* with Colleagues, Clients – A Story

Nets & Nettles Nest ~

What is your way of 'Being' with your colleagues even as you may be 'doing' many things individually, or collectively?

...

What senses do you become aware of when you enter a forest?

...

What do you notice/feel as you think of your colleagues?

...

What do you do in a forest?

...

What are your hopes and aspirations for your colleagues; the one who is your friend and the one who is a pain, for you?

...

What forest have you been thinking of all along? Is it safe?

...

Is practical spirituality or practice of *satsang* possible at workplace?

...

Imagine the Redwoods forest in California. I have not been there, yet, so I imagine the enchanted woods from one of Enid Blyton's books. She was one of my earliest, favourite authors. I believed without questioning that trees, animals and birds speak, and that adventure and magic are the keys to our lives. Then I grew up. Too fast!

Yet, I would return to the enchanted forests whenever I wanted to, when I was happy or sad, when I was disillusioned or clear and especially when anyone would say, 'it is a jungle out there'.

It was akin to a fairy tale when I found my dream job description on the net, applied and met the guardian of the Sequoia forest in Singapore, metaphorically speaking. Tan Shang How, Managing Director of Sequoia Consulting, passionately spoke to the vision and mission of his company, which had started as a sole proprietorship by the mother Sequoia tree and was on its verge of expanding. I felt like the Cheshire cat, grinning widely, after my interview where the forest guardian, akin to the wise caterpillar from Alice of Wonderland asked puffing good questions!

I was geared to take on whatever emerged in the forest/jungle, safe/not. High velocity, seeking direction, I was speeding against time, creating a storm in the forest, when I was given the direction to have patience.

Screeching brakes!

It reminded me of my teacher's words, 'Rome was not built in a day'. The Cheshire grin disappeared. 'Slow down' seemed to be an antithesis to success. I was told that was my mental model/mindset. I was introduced to the works of Systems Thinking, Learning Organization, Change Management, Strategic Planning and Leadership Development, except that it was all too slow, for me.

Shang would talk to me, which meant more questions that would perplex me. (Only years later when I accredited to be an executive coach, I realized that he was my coach informally all along and how crucial it is for good leadership to play the role of a coach!), The questions created a field of exploration and discovery, where I could play with my colleagues a good soccer game.

As a leader, Shang helped us pace, picking on our strengths deliberately and personally attending to the projects that we were undertaking.

It was unlike many leaders in organisations that my friends worked in, who were mostly absent or present only virtually, demanding updates on results. The result was that my friends would quit and chide me for being in my comfort zone.

But I was not! I was really uncomfortable and still learning in the Sequoia forest. Those questions were driving me mad. My colleagues and I would have our own mad-hatters party and conversations over *chai*. Then we would take action. I was uncomfortable and stretched to my limits, but in a safe way.

I was not in a jungle and Darwin's law was not at work. I was in a forest. It was a Sequoia forest. If you read how Sequoias thrive in nature, it is through a strong network of roots, which is invisible to the eye. One only sees the tall, individual trees standing strong.

Only months later did I realize that while Shang held the foundations strong gently, we played on the surface weathering all clients and standing tall in our laurels. He attended to the roots while we attended to the work, to strengthen the shoots – our client systems. He looked within the organisation while we looked without.

I wondered as a leader if he felt lonely and unseen. I did know that he had deep reserves of inspiration from soccer, Chinese philosophy, interpreting business in the 21st century with respect to the latest research, practising Leadership skills that we were teaching our clients.

Seriously, can anyone dare truly say that he/she is entirely self-made? If yes, then he/she needs to be introduced to how living systems and nature works.

I was in my natural element in Sequoia. Wishing to grow tall, fast, very fast, I pestered along with my questions, which was silenced with one in response, 'What do you want to create and what do you have?'

Over time, I learnt to differentiate between reactions and response; much as the differentiation between a forest and a jungle. There is wisdom in slowing down to restructure, engage and apply systems thinking. One can score more goals when the strategy, team, physical fitness and ambition are all in place.

The same lessons were reinforced for me as I learnt basic scuba diving. There is wisdom in understanding the route one intends to navigate, have reliable equipment, work in buddy system and be safe even when you are having fun.

Good leaders help create that safety net even while empowering and enabling. Sure, it may come across as a sting at the receiving end like a nettle. Nettles are essential herbs for diet, which is good when, served cooked/dried. While harvesting them though, they sting. The Sequoia forest felt like a net, safe, and restrictive.

Nets & Nettles.

The story continues.

If you inevitably spend a good number of hours at the workplace, what difference might it make to the quality of your life if you were to make that workplace peaceful and sacred for yourself, your colleagues and clients?

I had learnt my lesson well in my previous job as shared in the previous story. Colleagues became a conscious word for me. I had learnt to look at the person before looking at the role. I engaged the person to know of her/his dream before knowing of her/his job description. I had learnt well from other's mistakes and did not have to repeat them. I had encountered some really ineffective and disastrous leadership and colleagueship in other jobs before entering the Sequoia forest, and primarily, why I had been unable to nest! Some nets and nettles are not worth it. You choose your battles based on what do you truly care about?

Zafirah Mohamed, my colleague and it was only the two of us for a long time, were like two peas in a pod. We are both AIESECers, interested in sustainability, and share a good deal of virtues amongst us. We are both strong headed, strong willed and strongly believe in our work. We complement each other. Unlike peas, however, if two human beings are kept in a pod, they do not necessarily sit there serenely.

We made a really good team on good days and a ferociously bad one on bad days.

Any one's inner state of mind determined if the day would be a good day or a bad day. Our inner state of mind was determined by a need to perform on the job, a need to contribute meaningfully, a need for confidence as we entered areas of work unknown to us, a need to learn, to appreciate and be appreciated, a need to personalize the job description befitting our personalities, understanding it and doing it well. Our inner state of mind was also determined by how we thought others thought about us; be it the Directors, the clients, our family members, friends and each other too, as colleagues. Our inner state of mind was determined by change, by our own health, by our personalities, by things in our control, and by things not in our control. Our inner state of mind was determined by all the assumptions, judgments, presuppositions and emotions we held onto tightly.

And yes, all of that, cumulatively, determined our behaviour towards our work and if it would be a good day or a bad day!

Zafirah was yet another friend who had courageously stepped out of her comfort zone and possibly the comfort zone of her family and community members in taking up an internship in Pakistan through AIESEC. She is a good storyteller and has a world of stories to share of her days living in a different culture with other foreign expats. She had undergone similar experiences with family, friends and fellow travelers that I have shared. Hence, we both shared a commonality in our learning of life.

Despite that commonality, we struggled or celebrated each day in our work, open in our communication with each other of whether it was a day for war or for peace, dramatically speaking! Everybody got used to our 'battles'. Like true warriors, we would respectfully put down our swords to rest at sunset. This was a particular behaviour that served us well over time. It was our habit of conversations over *chai*. Like true colleagues-friends, we would head for some *chai* in the evenings, making sense of all that transpired with the clients, the work, our learning in relation to more stories of our personal lives. One day, after a workshop that was close to her home, we went to her home for *chai,* which was very good Pakistani tea that she made. On another day, after a workshop that was close to my home, we came to my home for *chai,* which was very good Darjeeling tea that also she made! Why?

I do not know how to make good *chai.* I mean, I do not have the patience for it. See, we learnt to leverage on our strengths.

Building on each other's strengths has to be a conscious practice. It can be done when both parties choose to focus on the strengths than the weaknesses. A lot of work in the inner world has to be done for that. Else, it is easy to forget and turn to war.

There was this time when we both stopped going out for *chai.* As soon as work got over, we both felt we needed our space and maybe could not bear to see each other. It was a very stressful phase. The surprising thing was that for the first time we were working on our dream project together, which we had to get it sanctioned from Shang, swimming across all those questions with credible good answers. The big day came. The event was a success.

Yet, something scarred remained between us.

Weeks went by where we both decided not to talk to each other.

However, that hardly helps. We could feel the chills of the cold war in sunny Singapore. More than that, we had learnt to care about each other. It mattered. Mustering courage to talk to her, I had to first find peace in my inner mind.

I put myself in her shoes and imagined what might her inner world be like, then? I recalled the stories of her passion, her contribution in Pakistan, her circumstances back in Singapore, how we came about this dream project, partnered together – wait, did we really partner and build on each others' strengths?

No.

Ah! Sweet nettles – even though you sting!

She had, meanwhile, put herself in my shoes and recalled my stories, purpose, meaning in life etc, or what she calls the importance of having a spiritual practice and to learn to let go of what does not serve. Her spiritual practices gave her courage to reflect, to take responsibility and spell out things exactly as they were – with her strengths and weaknesses and all, and also mine.

She knew that I was undertaking that dream project as a way to fulfill a loss in my personal life. She knew that not grieving or running away from the unaddressed emotions because of the personal losses was not healthy. She definitely knew that falling in a rabbit hole of a dream project even with the best of intentions could still cause one to be lost in the labyrinth of the forests in the deep psyche. This was something we had spoken about when she had done something similar after her father had passed away. As colleagues, we are gifted with great opportunities to mirror for each other safety and meaning even on a battlefield.

One evening, we finally said, 'let's connect.'

Over our next cup of tea, we shared with each other what we both had inkling about. Listening to each other and how we had stepped on to each other's boundaries/comfort zones was an affirmation. Just speaking authentically was therapeutic in itself. Sometimes what cannot be addressed with family and friends ripples out at the work place. It is blessed to have a good friend at the workplace.

Another life lesson – it is good to embody true warriorship for what you care about, attending to the Mission of the project but not to be caught unawares of the collateral damage caused.

We were soon able to rise above the scars not only of the dream project but also the deeper held ones, as we teamed up for yet another project. It circles back to 'Who are you?' and 'Who are you becoming?' and 'What is your awareness around that?' I realized I had momentarily slipped from the Cheshire cat grin into embodying the Red Queen from Alice of Wonderland, screaming 'off with their heads' in the excuse of my passion for the dream project.

Passion as an overdrive can burn the tires much like in the F1 races and that is when you need your team to replace the damage. As a team, it is essential to practice *satsang,* practice empathy, mindfulness, emotional intelligence, the art of having authentic conversations, tapping into the joy of rooting for each other's success and taking care of each other in failure and in learning.

In the world of competition and strife that advocates separation of identity, what might respecting a deeper identity serve where each one wishes to do fulfilling work, serve well and be seen well in the eyes of our colleagues, worthy of our commitment?

Seeing the sameness beyond the separateness, we felt proud to have co-created this culture for our company and a strong container where we welcomed new colleagues. Any culture has an impact on new colleagues who join. Our evolving culture was further nurtured by the best of our new colleagues.

Nets & Nettles Nest.

'Look beyond a person's weaknesses to access her/his strengths', Minister Lim Swee Say, one of our clients had shared this in his leadership lens on Organisation Development for the Labour Union. We learnt from our clients.

'Develop your own style in your work. Develop your heart. Write, if that is your dream. Write for your dreams. Write in your dreams', Serene, one of our adjunct coaches, naturally mentored me. Like the White Queen from Alice of Wonderland, her caring questions or counsels would be like believing "six impossible things before breakfast". We learn from our partners.

'Sequoia forest is a living system, practicing living OD.' We learn from nature and natural laws.

I hope and pray for you that you find your community of nets and nettles. There will always be restrictions and stings but are they worth it for you and your vision to nest and grow what is life giving. I trust you to practice nurturing your nurturing skills for yourself and others, to become the best of who each one is supposed to be.

Never say never!

Grandma

PS: So, my loving grandchildren, what are your stories of life's nimble lessons from nature, from your own and others' nature or natural way of being, for your *Practice of Satsang*, in your times?

"Life's just too short to be sitting around waiting for things to happen."

-Zafirah Mohamed (2014)
-(*My Colleague, Co-Trouble-Maker*, Senior Consultant)

"How do we behave and make decisions in ways that the people around us,
whether they are our clients or colleagues or partners,
feel that they have been valued, have learned and have
experienced the positive energy radiated from within us?"

Tan Shang How (2014)
(Managing Director, Sequoia Group Pte Ltd)

Now, it is time for Practice.
You may create your own or experiment with one I suggest below.

Practice
(N)

To practice saying NO to what does not serve, and strengthening the net and nest of relationships.

- Note the strengths, life-stories, context of your colleagues of all that is shared, all that you hear and all that you observe.
- While working with the same, when you encounter a weakness that has an impact on you and your work, deliberately recall the strengths, life-stories and context of that colleague before you react.
- Speak to the truth of the weakness in light of that context, concentrating on how to improve, learn and be effective together.
- You always have the gift of gratitude available to you. Anytime when the net or nest is under threat of breaking, recall the essence for which you are grateful to your colleague, over and over again, in your inner world.

PS: It is helpful to recall yours and others strengths often, repetitively, aligning them to address the many problems at work. It is also helpful to learn and challenge yours and others weaknesses kindly. The magic of Gestalt!

On sight and insight ~

~ Letters to my grandchildren ~

My dear little ones, out of the many words you will learn starting with the alphabet 'O', I have a few fundamental ones to share. In addition to 'Owl' or 'Oats', words that helped me to understand the world, the outer world, I was curious to gain access to the mysterious inner world that exists within us. The secret to peace, happiness and fulfillment lies in there. Our inner world determines how we respond to the outer world - people, places and perspectives. Practicing the essence of the few fundamental words below has been life-giving, nourishing and key to expanding possibilities for me

As you grow each day into beautiful beings, I invite you to experiment, play and discover the essence of these words in your life. As you master the game, you will get clues to master your life and create your own future that is meaningful, day-by-day. The key is to choose wisely and practice consciously. Remember, whatever you practice; consciously, sub-consciously, or unconsciously, right or wrong, it grows stronger. So, what do you choose?

O for Ontological Open-mindedness

- What is your practice of observing your own thoughts, and others' thoughts; in relation to each other? Do they build on each other from a learning frame, or clash against each other, so one has to be thrown away that does not fit your frame?
- What is your way of being in the different roles & positions you acquire at work?

O for Ownership

- What are the values you own and practice in your 10s, 20s, 30s, 50s, 70s .. so on?
- What are you ready to let go of?

O for Om and Omnipresence

- What is your spiritual centeredness for your work, success and sustainability?
- What is your mindset of service towards people and the planet, even if you are a profit-business owner?

Other words, still starting with 'O', also served me but only for short-term. Practice of the essence of these words fed my ego and exhausted me in the long-term as I found them to be life-depleting;

O for 'Oppressive', 'Overworked' and 'Outraged out of habit with no action'

Practice of *Satsang* with Colleagues, Clients – A Story

On sight and insight ~

'During my time, we learnt things the hard way. The younger generation gets it easy.'

'Why do they keep coming to me for answers? They ought to think for themselves.'

'I only meet with silence when I ask a question, so I cannot help but give the answer. Leadership is so difficult.'

'The culture of our organisation is poisonous. We have high attrition, low productivity, politics and a lot of unhappiness.'

'We are no longer relevant. The competition is strong.'

'We do not have vision. We do not have money. We do not have resources. We do not have time.'

'We have an open door policy but a lot of dealings are made behind closed doors.'

'Our culture needs a make-over.'

'We have vision which is visible only on paper.'

'Our education system is outdated. Our healthcare is not life giving. Our businesses are killing people.'

'I give my best but I am not seen, not heard and not appreciated. I am tired and uninspired.'

'I/We have tried everything to solve this problem. It still persists.'

'I/We are sick of this culture of fear that prevails. It is stressful.'

My work with my clients, who may be individuals, teams or organisations, makes me see a lot of problems that I could have never ever imagined. The problems are wicked, complex, heartless and hopeless. It is only then that most clients would seek consultants, pretty much as when people seek doctors for cure after their self-medication has failed. Truth be told, I am the best imperfect example for the latter, much to the chagrin of my family doctor.

To continue with the analogy, pretty much, most of the clients hope for the magic pill to take care of the problem, forgetting that pills address symptoms at best.

As part of my work, it is my work hence to remind them of the larger field than the one that they see.

Seeing. Sight. Vision. It all boils down to that.

When we seek help from another, be it professionally or personally, what we are truly seeking is the key to open the door of that insight which brings the solution on sight.

Insight is the key.

If insight is the key, what attributes serve for individual and collective insights at workplaces to be seen, heard and acted from?

Who are your teachers, in your personal, professional or spiritual lives who have helped you gain insights, just as you may have helped others gain insights, naturally?

There is a world of resources out there to learn from. Yet, the resources serve in expanding and broadening knowledge. Insight and experiences deepen the field into your wisdom and knowing, which no one can take away from you.

Many professionals seek experiences from different landscapes of the larger field; social development sector, private sector, public sector, emerging new sectors that cannot be defined in a narrow way and so on and so forth.

I had started with the social development sector where one of the key treasures cutting across the differences was the attribute of 'Engaging the stakeholders'. The sector is full of stories of the brave souls who travel to the farthest villages/points in the psyche to engage and educate and be educated. Across international waters, one reinforcing phenomenon soon came to light. Only those solutions continued to thrive that had tapped on to the insights of the diverse stakeholders, who then owned the work. Having had inspiring colleagues, friends and teachers from that world, I had incubated some of the core values without even realising it, early on in my career. Years after, when I was working in the same field albeit from a different direction and stake, the insights gleaned from the past helped the future we wished to create. On sight with my team with a client group who were keen to get clarity on their strategies and direction, the incubation helped emerge a crazy idea that had not been tried or tested.

A group of passionate and seasoned adults were our client group whose purpose was to serve a certain sector of children. Child centric is often the theme in schools, NGOs, certain communities and advocacy groups. Imagining their future, and hence their services, all that the client group could see were obstacles, barriers and complaints by the children. After a while, I found my field of vision narrowing down too as we focused on the challenges and the cul de sacs.

Later, our team were looking at the data and trying to see where the breakthrough might be, when we suddenly had a collective insight – we had no data from the children themselves! We only had a sense of some of their complaints but definitely did not have the full story of where they might be coming from and why. The solution was simple – which the clients discovered themselves, once we worked on our insight of engaging the children through processes that would help engage their whole selves. The children were pleasantly surprised on being involved and participated whole-heartedly. Their insights and things that were on sight for them helped the adults gain clarity around strategies and direction. Not only that, some of the children stepped up to help with some of the implementation work. Ownership and trust was built.

In a leadership workshop overseas, as a participant, this insight was reinforced by the story of impacting positive education in a school, a much dire need explored by Singapore's education system as well. The story-tellers shared their insight of including students in the conversations with school leaders, teachers and parents.

I learnt a deeper lesson there to trust our insights, the spiritual wholeness versus engaging the minds alone to create spaces for breakthroughs and creativity. I remembered how mad I was when I would perceive that my life decisions were being taken by my grandparents and parents without involving me. Culturally, it was even appropriate and safe in those times. Yet, I had rebelled simply because my insights and views had felt neglected. There is much we can learn from personal lives about professional engagement and vice versa.

For many of the problems shared above, once we helped our diverse clients from different sectors tap into their higher consciousness, aspirations and hopes, they reframed the problems with awareness as follows -

'We had our own struggles and the younger generation has theirs. We have to listen to them to find out how we can help, or not. It is their learning curve.'

'We need to help people find answers who are searching for them. Let us share information and think innovatively.'

'I have to change the way I ask questions and understand what it takes to break the culture of silence. Leadership is about creating trust and enabling capabilities.'

'The culture of our organisation is what we made it. We are committed to change and build an appreciative, enabling and engaging culture, prioritizing our people's needs because they matter.'

'We love the competition. It keeps us alive, forces us to learn and stay relevant. However, let us stick to honestly healthy competition to bring out personal bests.'

'Let us be aligned in our purpose. With a compelling one, we will find money and resources and time to do our work.'

'We have an open door policy and practices that encourage alignment of intentions and behaviours.'

'We make our culture.'

'We have to align everything to co-create our vision.'

'Our education system has passionate teachers and administrators, new-age eager students, educated parents. We just need to engage them all to improve the system. Our healthcare has good clinicians, constantly learning cutting edge ways and research. Our businesses' soul needs to be tapped on.'

'I give my best and that is priceless. I know I make a difference and inspire others. I do not need approval from others. I gauge, give and receive feedback and have my pulse on the pulse of things. This is my indicator of happiness.'

'If we have not solved the problem, there is still something to be learnt, to be born.'

Well, what is your story?

Do you tend to the problems or are you on the bandwagon of reframed lenses?

Whichever it might be, hard work and heart work is required.

However, I have observed that with clients and teams who are centered on values, are open minded to work both on their strengths and shadow sides, watch out for each other and their purpose, the solutions are surprising, renewing and far-reaching with positive results. The whole system can optimize on conscious practices at workplaces to create the desired results.

A lot of the stories of problems or opportunities exist in the inner worlds and may or may not be representative factually of the outer world. I meet people with an attitude of abundance and even with meager salaries, long hours of work, they still manage to find the sun's energy of optimism and opportunities in the worse case scenarios. Other people have an attitude of scarcity and even the real sun cannot get them out of their own inner darkness and feeling of lacking. Many of us alternate in our moods amidst the two "realities".

Ontological shifts.

For years, I was stuck in certain ways of thinking and story-telling between the two "realities". The roots went deep in my psyche where I had little or no access at times. The roots even went deep in my family space and personal space that had nothing to do with my work. Yet, I carried my body, mind and spirit influenced by certain ways of thinking into my work place. My feeling of getting stuck and refusal to shape up left others feeling stuck. Slowly, we became a big body of being stuck together.

As thought leaders and *teachers,* often we noticed that even when we changed the thoughts in our heads, somehow, there was a civil war between the mind and the body! My favourite simple example – irrespective of buying the most charming alarm clock, thinking of waking up early and exercising and even asking a friend to wake me up, my body would simply not listen. 'It' has broken many alarm-clocks over the years until I stopped buying alarm-clocks and use the one on the iPhone. Somehow, 'It' has stopped itself from throwing the iPhone in the semi-sleep state!

The key to getting unstuck is when we truly reflect, act, take risks and learn from a person first-person perspective than a second or third person perspective. Learning about Ontology, the philosophical study of the nature of being, becoming, existence and experience and relations, helped me reframe and get unstuck for layers that had seemed frozen in my being. It also helped me work effectively with my clients who once unstuck, carry forward the gift of this consciousness, irrespective of their roles.

It is true work - Mind-over-body and body-over-mind! It is worth it. The souls of all the alarm-clocks would agree. It is a matter of time and space when either we choose to stoke the fires or the fire consumes us.

Optimize on optimism.

I believed that other people carry a fire too which sometimes gets dimmed in the face of abstract darkness. Listening to stories of Deepavali (the Indian festival of lights) from my grandmother as a child, I had learnt to light up one candle with another and to be persistent at it, even if some burnt out. The deeper story was to work with the darkness within and without, of self and others and towards light and life.

When I entered the workplace field, with a lot of rumoured stories of 'it' being a dark place, I just believed that all one had to do individually and collectively was to work with the darkness and look for that spark of light/insight. If we constantly lit up the lives of our colleagues and clients, there would be little or no burn out! (Pun intended)

Spending around/more than eight hours at work, it is insane to believe in the worst of the stories, carry that stress in the heads and the hearts, (which has the worst impact on our bodies) and pretend not to feel anything in the act of being professional. I cannot imagine being devoid of a good friend at the workplace, operating under competition and continuing to work meeting deadlines after deadlines.

Till date, I have not found a single client who has that insane imagination either. Everyone has hopes and aspirations. Some have more resentment and resigned feelings around things that will not change or things that have changed. Yet, with some self-work, support from structures and processes and others, one has the innate ability to feel one's inner light. Some take more time than others, caught up in the ancient works of freeze, fight or flight! But once brought to their sight, their own insights can free them.

Who calls for the pink elephant where the stakes are high? Many conscious leaders are practising creating safe and trusting environment where the different ranks and files share freely what they see differently as the proverbial three blind men who attempt to 'see' the elephant.

Some transformational courageous and healing work is possible in organisations that have an impact on education, healthcare, national economies, developmental sector, profit oriented business which routes back the earnings to where it matters. If one cares for it, there are many stories out there to learn from, contextualize and draw further insights from.

What is on your sight when you think of spirituality at the workplace?

What are your insights about transformational professionalism to serve the wealth of resources; people, planet and peace?

Who are you - A carrier of light or darkness?

I hope and pray for you that you find the right friends at your workplace who help to evoke insight and to help you keep the right goals on sight. I trust you to practice open-mindedness, owning your values and skills to tap on collective insights and help bring light and life to self and others.

O my!

Grandma

PS: So, my lovely grandchildren, what are your stories where you have ontologically shifted people and processes from darkness to light at work as your *Practice of Satsang*, in your times?

"Stay connected to what is important to you.
Stay connected to what makes your heart beat faster thinking about it.
Stay connected to nature and listen deeply. Stay connected to family."

-Wendy Koh (2014)
-(My colleague & A Lover of life)

Now, it is time for Practice.
You may create your own or experiment with one I suggest below.

Practice
(O)

To be aware of your own state of being and the relations you have with yourself, your inner world and others in your outer world.

- EVERY DAY, before entering the workplace, carve out 5 minutes to remember a truly invaluable value or purpose that is meaningful for you.
    - o Think of an anchoring story or moment when you were in a state of being that was fearless, inspiring, caring and trusting that is meaningful to you.
    - o Create a personal artifact that reminds you of the essence of being.
    - o Pick a set of cards/treasure that speak to you and that you can hold for the brief moment if that helps.
- Breathe in deeply in your belly to connect with your soul.
- Now enter the workplace knowing that you can respond to everything and everyone that comes your way.
- After you finish work, before leaving the workplace, carve out 5 minutes to revisit the same value or purpose and think of any one instance during the day when you showed up at work BEING an embodiment of that value. (Example: you can read about kindness or you can BE kind.)

o   Incase you cannot narrow down to a moment and feel that you did not embody, worry not. You still have the evening with your loved ones or with yourself to practice that.

PS: Notice over time what shifts for you and others? What surprises you? What touches you?

Poison or Peace? What are you Present to? ~

~ Letters to my grandchildren ~

My dear little ones, out of the many words you will learn starting with the alphabet 'P', I have a few fundamental ones to share. In addition to 'Play' or 'Pull/Push', words that helped me to understand the world, the outer world, I was curious to gain access to the mysterious inner world that exists within us. The secret to peace, happiness and fulfillment lies in there. Our inner world determines how we respond to the outer world - people, places and perspectives. Practicing the essence of the few fundamental words below has been life-giving, nourishing and key to expanding possibilities for me

As you grow each day into beautiful beings, I invite you to experiment, play and discover the essence of these words in your life. As you master the game, you will get clues to master your life and create your own future that is meaningful, day-by-day. The key is to choose wisely and practice consciously. Remember, whatever you practice; consciously, sub-consciously, or unconsciously, right or wrong, it grows stronger. So, what do you choose?

P for Presence

- What difference does your presence make and to whom, or for what? Or, alternatively, your impact does your absence have?
- What do you practice to be present in the now, for somebody/something that matters, and let go of the past hurt and memories or even future dreams and distractions?

P for Purpose, Play & Peace

- What values do you practice to bring purpose, play and peace in life?
- What are your skills to help another see purpose, uplifting play energy and find peace in the face of hopelessness and helplessness?

P for Planet

- What do you do in everyday living to take care of the planet?
- What do you see beyond the daily strife and petty obsessions of the ego to be able to be part of the universal process?

Other words, still starting with 'P', also served me but only for short-term. Practice of the essence of these words fed my ego and exhausted me in the long-term as I found them to be life-depleting;

P for 'Poisonous', 'Paranoid' and 'Petty'.

Practice of *Satsang* with Colleagues, Clients – A Story

Poison or Peace? What are you Present to? ~

Professional.	Personal.	Positive.
People.	Profit.	Planet.
Power.	Powerless.	Position.
Precise.	Playful.	Possibilities.
Pragmatic.	Practical.	Philosophical.
Polarity.	Polaroid.	Platonic.
Physics.	Prayer.	Philanthropy.
Physical.	Pretty.	Presence.
Persevering	Pain-averse	Prying.
Purist.	Perceptive.	Peaceful.
Personalities.	Process.	Purpose.
Practice.	Practice.	Practice.

Pick the constructs that you identify with and embody it in your field of work.

Pick the constructs that you do not resonate with, and avoid it in your field of work.

Pick the constructs that you are a complete stranger to.

Pick the constructs that you are indifferent to.

Remember, whatever you practice; consciously, sub-consciously, or unconsciously, right or wrong, it grows stronger. So, what do you choose?

Why do you choose that? What is your earliest memory of learning that?

Why do you conform for some constructs and avoid others?

When did you learn/unlearn that construct? Who was your role model for it?

Do you find yourselves balancing or seeking balance?

Do you feel whole?

What is missing?

Constructs are just concepts that can be utilized as lenses or thought bubbles to bring peace or to poison an idea, a way of being, a group of people or an organisation.

Constructs are constructed socially in our social brain and may be interpreted differently. They are best explained through stories and experienced through being present to them.

Working with various people from various sectors, I have always enjoyed discovering the stories behind which people choose their choice of subject and field of work based on the liking or aversion of some of the above constructs. I have witnessed people of all ages and types enjoy discovering who they are. They often wonder about their choices, conscious or not, on who they wish to be when they realize how their choice of subject or field of work exposes them to only some of the constructs. Every field of subject and work has certain biasness towards and against different constructs and therefore, demands conformity/capability.

A common example of 'living a good life' construct is to do well in school, then university, then job, then get married, have children and then teach the children the same. An uncommon example of 'living a good life' construct is to balance studies with creativity and consciousness in school, cultivate a hobby, travel and discover self in university, work well and take a break from the job every now and then without fearing scarcity of bank balance, have a learning partner whom you love and marry and have children with. By the way, you bring up the children with freedom who may choose the opposite of what you have. But it is ok. What matters is the relationship and not the qualifications and goals alone. What matters is the living than the obsession with the good life!

As soon as one enters a profession or organisation, the culture whispers the constructs that are seen favourably. The common whispers of cultures are often caught and interpreted pretty accurately by little children.

Often young children are asked, what will you become when you grow up?

These days, I hear many of them say, 'I will earn lots of money when I grow up.'

I ask some of them, 'what will you do with the lots of money?'

Some of them say they will buy more dresses, shoes and cars.

Others say that they do not know.

In rare cases, I have heard one or two of them say that they will give it to mummy – papa! I once heard a little one say that with lots of money, she will not have to work.

I looked at her mother, who looked at me with pleading eyes. It is wonderful to learn of constructs through the eyes of children. It directly mirrors what cultures value most and rings with the uncomfortable truth of times.

My biggest discomfort has been with the idea of dividing myself into personal and professional halves! I have always felt that to be like an amputation of my self. Unable to withstand the pain of it, I realized how professionalism silently tip-toed itself in my personal relations. My ways of being became one of rigidity, safe-guardedness and caution. I could not see anything wrong with the construct I was living in. It was only when the stress multiplied to the extent of threatening my health that I woke up from the slumber. Whatever had happened to my dreams? What was I present to and absent to?

My clients, at a given time, from education and healthcare sectors had a similar awakening after I probed them with questions and stories. Most of their stories circulated around getting so busy in life with their presence only for the next problem to be fixed or the next fire to be doused. Conveniently, they forgot individually and collectively to be present to their dreams, their vision, their values and the important part of the work. I learnt from many of them in their mid-life crisis phases to question the constructs of productivity or profit-making that is sold to us en masse.

One of the biggest lessons learnt was to be wary of the poison of 'self-aggrandizement'. Many professionals who wished focused on nurturing their 'baby' at work alone were left stranded nearing retirement age or transfer. The power of competition is another construct often over-rated. Caught in this poisonous rat race, one loses one's peace of mind that is essential for the real work one aspires to do.

Another lesson was to be wary of 'money-money-money' as the foundation for all happiness. Little doubt that in my times consumerism is at its peak.. Many people cannot talk about money in a healthy manner, be it with their families or at the workplaces. There is a lot of emphasis on the value of money. Yet, people also value the mystical happiness. Interestingly, some manage to fall in between the gaps and strike lottery! They strike a happy balance with the truth of who they are, what their profession brings to them and what they tend to make out of their lives.

Who are your role models either from your field of work or another?

Uncomfortable with dividing my true self into a false professional self and a true personal self, I naturally orbited towards what I had observed since my childhood. I had always read and heard that doctors were taught to be objective, which meant truly dividing the personal from the professional. I knew many who would conform. However, the one doctor whom I met most frequently was one who had escaped from the net of forced constructs. He is my family doctor, Dr Tapan Chatterjee. He is always relational with his patients. He spends time listening to their life stories than symptoms alone. The former, many a time, helps in the healing of the patients more than the medicines given to treat the symptoms. Even now, he attends to fewer patients, especially those who cannot pay very well. He calls it his retirement plan to serve the community in his own way. The way I see it, he has always served judging by the strong queue of patients waiting for hours to see him, to enjoy the brief conversation of life, and Life with him!

Doctors hold a credible position in many societies and communities. I have seen some of them advocate passionately for well-being than the fix and cure model of healthcare. At the risk of losing many a patient, some still do not pander to the politics of mayhem in healthcare at the cost of patients.

Success is another construct that we shape and that shapes us.

What are your indicators of success?

Success meant good grades for a student and the number of students who got good grades for a teacher. Yet, the best of the teachers (and I qualify best by their ability to win the trust of students) in my school days emphasized upon the type of education and character building that would earn the favours of a serving life, worthy of remembrance. Those teachers brought out the best in every child, raising them to their next personal best level. As students, we doted on those teachers and as a result of that, worked extra hard for the subjects they taught us. Little surprise that we got good results in those papers. It is a virtuous cycle. If this is the law of positive education, wonder how come all educators do not see this?

What do you value in your work?

In many workplaces that was influenced by positive psychology and strengths based approaches, I saw people valued individuality at work. People-oriented professionals were present to caring and empowering the teams in the organisations. Process-oriented professionals were present to improving the structures and flow that would lead to better productivity. Purpose-oriented professionals were present to preserving the core and sharpening the learning edge that would serve the purpose. Politics-oriented professionals were present to the resentment and resignation and ensured to use them as their means to achieve their own ends. Paranoid-oriented professionals always made decisions based on the construct of fear.

Poison or Peace – What are you Present to?

When people align their true selves with the constructs that bring out the best in them, they thrive in their work. When people align their masked selves with

204

constructs that must/should be, they experienced an inner pull and tension that was divisive in nature. Learning from Physics and the law of hologram, it is essential to reflect on the constructs one unquestioningly adopts and see if that serves or if it has become irrelevant?

Here is a stark imagery. If most professionals were given the choice to administer real poison to their fellow-colleagues and clients, many would not do so. Peace rules!

However, if most professionals lost in the labyrinth of their identity and attached to their positions were given the choice to administer real poison to fellow human beings, many might just do so! Poison rules!

Little wonder, many work fields in the world in my times are mini replicas of the battlefields. At the same time, conscious and conscientious warriors are constantly at work too creating a powerful presence of purpose and values, be it the public sector, social sector, entrepreneurial sector and even in some parts of the private sector.

Older patterns of consciousness and presence only towards surviving are slowly giving way to newer patterns and practices of consciousness and presence towards thriving. Organisations, stakeholders and communities are willing to work applying latest research around efficiency, organizational development and productivity.

Many organisations are beginning to mean it when they say people are their resources. Although politically and economically, things might appear to have shifted little, a lot of people are exposed to current social realities working across generations and cultures today.

The presence of people in virtual and real spaces are observed and experienced viscerally. One can almost sniff the constructs different people adhere to. Vulnerability, trust, care and compassion seem to be the new cry even at workplaces amongst colleagues, clients and partners. Newer generation in the workforce refuse to give the same importance to affirmations for working very diligently at the cost of one's self-care. Many in the new generation are also not as attached to safety measures and bank balance accounts. They yearn to experience life in the broader spectrum. The good news is that real, authentic and meaningful work is possible today.

I hope and pray for you that you choose role models and learn to appreciate peace in your inner world and in your relationships in life. I trust you to practice courage and compassion to challenge poisonous elements that do not serve the people, the planet and the purpose of conscious living.

Primarily yours,

Grandma

PS: So, my loving grandchildren, what are your stories of being present to peace for your *Practice of Satsang*, in your times?

"How can Story serve positive systemic shift in our world?"

Mary Alice Arthur (2014)
-(Global Story teller, Harvester,
Creator for processes that bring forth stories,
heal with stories and change the future with stories,
My Inspiring Role Model &Teacher)

Now, it is time for Practice.
You may create your own or experiment with one I suggest below.

Practice
(P)

To enjoy the truth in your own story and the story of others.

- Share your story through any medium that you desire.
- Listen to others' stories as they believe in it.
- Listen to your inner voice: How can your or others' story serve as a positive and generative shift for yourself and others?

PS: Tell more stories.

PART
5

Practice of *Satsang* with Community

Quintessential Questions ~

~ Letters to my grandchildren ~

My dear little ones, out of the many words you will learn starting with the alphabet 'Q', I have a few fundamental ones to share. In addition to 'Queen' or 'Quiz', words that helped me to understand the world, the outer world, I was curious to gain access to the mysterious inner world that exists within us. The secret to peace, happiness and fulfillment lies in there. Our inner world determines how we respond to the outer world - people, places and perspectives. Practicing the essence of the few fundamental words below has been life-giving, nourishing and key to expanding possibilities for me

As you grow each day into beautiful beings, I invite you to experiment, play and discover the essence of these words in your life. As you master the game, you will get clues to master your life and create your own future that is meaningful, day-by-day. The key is to choose wisely and practice consciously. Remember, whatever you practice; consciously, sub-consciously, or unconsciously, right or wrong, it grows stronger. So, what do you choose?

Q for 'Qi'

- What do you change in yourself to honour and uplift the Qi/*chi*/natural energy/life force/*prana* in others?
- What do you practice to honour your own Qi and recognize its presence?

Q for 'Questioning'

- What beliefs in yourself or others do you question? Why, and why not?
- What questions are you asking yourself, and which questions are you avoiding?

Q for 'Quality'

- Do you recognize the quality of yours and others' 'higher and lower self' in one's thoughts, emotions and actions?

- What would you compromise quality for?

Other words, still starting with 'Q', also served me but only for short-term. Practice of the essence of these words fed my ego and exhausted me in the long-term as I found them to be life-depleting;

Q for 'Quarrelsome', 'Quick-tempered' and 'Queasy'.

Practice of *Satsang* with Community – A Story

Quintessential Questions ~

Notice yourself in conversations.

Do you end up sharing a lot of information, resources, giving advice, and telling more than asking? Also, if you ask questions, what kind of questions do you ask? Are they the commonplace ones as 'how are you' or are they more specific customized for the person you are talking to? Of course in order to be customized, one has to have a good relation with the person to really know what to ask! Also are the questions critical or are they questions that serve criticism? Or, are the questions competitive in nature, asked not out of curiosity but to make a point, much like a win-lose situation?

How I wished I knew how to ask the precise questions in the precise acid-dripping tone when I was training to be a young debater in school! I was said to be eloquent in my speech delivery, with good clarity and pronunciation, bringing in impressive facts and aspects in a debate. However, I would freeze in the 'rebuttal' rounds, a minute given after each speaker has presented to critique/question the opposition's point of view. I would end up asking 'not so powerful' questions because sometimes they veered towards a win-win situation.

The point was driven home when I lost in the final round, once. It haunted me as the pain point for a long time and I had difficulty letting go of that memory. I had been kind because I had found some merit in what my opposition was saying and had asked a 'silly' question of considering that point in relation to a point I had made. My favourite expression then would be to bring a germ of an idea (much like an amoeba) to the table and for others to build upon that germ into any living organism. In a debate, however, this principle does not serve.

Someone from the audience (one of the opposition's friends) screamed that I agree with him and have hence lost my case! All his other friends laughed. I wanted to clarify but my time was up. Why are we always running against

213

time to be listened to? Some of my fellow-debaters would hence speak really fast. Impressive as it looked, it did not serve most children from the school who would 'switch off'. The point of learning was then lost.

On that fateful event, listening to the laughter of the opposition part of the audience, I had a sinking feeling in my stomach as I retreated. I wish I had just one more chance to be heard. But there was only one rebuttal round for each speaker. It was the opposition's turn. Then he appeared, my worthy opposition. Looking at his friends, half-winking at them, he swaggered to the podium and said something about disagreeing with me and landed his fist forcefully on the podium to stress upon that. The boys in the audience mimicked his behaviour and began to cheer and clap and create a din.

At that precise moment, I wished the ground would swallow me up, or that I could just disappear. I felt like the loser. The sinking feeling turned to a drowning feeling. Even though I stood composed, I was dying within, waiting for the judges to give their verdict. Suddenly, I had a powerful question. 'Did his friends even 'listen' to him, or did they just 'look' at him to decide the fate of our debate?

Time passed by slowly, painfully. After a full five minutes, the head judge walked up to the podium and announced that the opposition school had won! I had lost. I had let my school down. Why did I have to see the merit in the other speaker?!! My schoolteacher joined me and with a sad smile said that the difference in the points that decided our fate was minimum. It made me feel worse. My schoolteacher further said that I was too gentle. But we are taught to be gentle in school. It is a virtue. Why was I punished for that?

I could not breathe. I still stood tall. I saved my last breath to walk up to the opposition candidate and congratulate him, who also congratulated me back warmly. He had a disarming smile. Our friends rushed to our respective sides. He was obviously liked by his mates. They were not evil after all. They were just schoolchildren like us.

Why do schools teach us how to have a debate, but does not teach us how to have a dialogue and build upon each other's ideas? Competition, instead of collaboration, charismatic looks and brash behaviour, instead of deep listening seemed to be the basis of a debating culture, I said in sad fury to my friends. One of them began to say something and I cut her off, by banging on the table and shouting, I disagree! Then I looked at her, she was taken aback, and asked her if I was effective. We laughed, and I finally cried, a little.

Years later in college life, I was relating the same story to my friends when we were watching the Indian Parliament in action. Much animated, watching our animated politician leaders, we spoke of democracy, leadership and values. What might be required for a community and country to grow? Even after debating for hours, we could not reach any consensus. We felt everything to be a lacking and soon went down a downward spiral of conversation.

Then, somebody asked what served to be a powerful question, 'What might be required for youth to grow? And in order to answer that without getting into rhetoric, reflect on what is missing in Your life that you wish you had more of to help you grow?' One had to speak from a personal point of view. Soon the debate turned to a dialogue as one began to share and reflect on what one had, what was not enough and what was most important.

As we tuned in to each other's stories, and listened for a change, we soon narrowed down to aspects that were the real obstacles to our growth. It was not just the money and the resources, for even though they are very important for growth, there are other more fundamental aspects that lead to the true growth and transformation of a person, community or country. What was missing was the fundamental values and clarity of wise management of the money and resources. It suddenly became clear that a blaming culture, a revengeful culture, a culture that puts an individual before a group cannot sustain growth. What was worse was that we were living in the old divisive ways of the majority and the minority. It was a perpetuating win-lose situation, much like in a debate.

We chose three aspects that would allow communities to thrive if they nurtured those.

The first aspect was truly skills for questioning to understand than to condemn. In most of our communities, those that we were born into, our school communities, local communities, we were made to be recipients where knowledge and wisdom was "told" to us. Most of us were discouraged from asking questions lest it should be interpreted as showing disrespect. Very rarely, few teachers or elders would pause and inquire for our contexts and help us sense-make. More rarely so, fewer teachers or elders would encourage and entertain the questions asked by the youth.

Whose duty is it to ask for fundamental, purposeful questions that help the community to reflect, stay relevant and respond to changing times? Who all are involved, or not?

The second aspect, perhaps as important as the first one, was simple listening skills. As children of even the smartest of businessmen, lawyers, doctors, most of the youth grew up with a feeling of not being listened to! The more we reflected, the more we saw the gap of listening skills in communities where again hierarchy is established inexplicitly for the older members to tell their wisdom and for the younger members to receive it by way of listening. With the rare exception of few elders, who would truly listen and encourage the children to share their stories, the majority of the people did not. Interestingly, children learn by observation and can easily spot the gap in what is being said and what is truly practiced. When they wish to speak up, the common experience was of being cut off. In these busy times, one does not have adequate time and space to truly share one's thought process as if we are all in an eternal platform of debate with just one rebuttal round, that determines the fate!

What do children observe growing up watching their family members, teachers, successful, famous people, the media, and politicians in a community?

The third aspect is the alignment of thoughts, words and actions to the values that matters. It is the alignment of understanding something intelligently with the practice of it. One informs the other. It is intertwined much as the DNA that defines the human species. For example, one can read about the value of humanity and kindness and understand it, or like the double helix, one can both read and be kind!

What might it look like if communities, individuals and collectives chose to both understand and practice conscious living and *satsang*?

216

The culture is formed by the patterns of what a community values and has much impact on the individuals and collectives of the culture. Some are aware of it. Some are not even aware. More often than not, the impact of a culture is felt most by the youth who are born into the community. The youth may not have consciously chosen or co-created the culture and hence is prone to asking quintessential questions. Atleast the potential is there, and with the right guidance and listening ear, some of those questions can truly serve, multi-generationally and multi-culturally.

It is far better than the questions most of the youth observed their families and community members ask of each other, 'Have you put on weight?' or 'Have you lost weight?' Other questions were 'status' questions, or even 'gossip' questions, or 'political' questions, or those that pertain to facts and figures.
With Google and social media becoming stronger in my times, many of the fact finding, knowledge questions turned into tapping fingers on tablets to search for answers. It is interesting to note the shift in conversations again.

Today, most questions are answered by 'Google it'. In the past, those who had knowledge, had power. A decade ago, the family sat together in the living room with their attention directed to the television under the threat of a war of the remote. Whoever had the remote in hand, had power. Today, people sit together in a common place, or even journey together in public transport with most of the eyes on their individual tablets and ears hidden by individual ear plugs. Conversations have turned into sharing resources and links, more often than not, even silently across the virtual world. Children, as young as toddlers, are attached to their tablets for learning and entertainments purposes. It is the new toy.

Each phase and generation has its pros and cons, opportunities and challenges. Yet, some things remain constant. Good questions prove to be more powerful than answers.

Who is there to ask the fundamental questions in a community to help collectively reflect on the pros and cons and hence make wise choices? Is it Education sector's job? Or, is it the job of politicians? Perhaps, industrialists and businessmen!

There are always those people who choose differently. They choose not to look away. They choose to create something if nothing exists. They choose to volunteer and be part of that something bigger in life that contributes to the well-being of the community. They may not have the answers and hence ask questions to engage other members of all ages. I have witnessed many a superhero in the garb of a caring person, who puts her/his life lesson learnt to well use.

I met Bernise Ang one fine day. Her story was as is often said in Singapore, 'same same but different'. She shared her memories of her experiences of feeling stifled and moulded by school and by the society. Like many youths, she felt valued not so much for who she was but for credentials, qualifications and grades. Silently, the experience found a comfort spot of feeling disempowered and uncared for, if one tries to put it in words. However, her experience was very different in an overseas education, where along with her friends, she was able to influence policies regarding internationals students. On returning to Singapore, what had become clearer was her calling to create an opportunity for youth in Singapore. She promised to get out of her comfort zone and helps others do the same. She believes in empowerment and caring. She wants her team to feel cared for, valued, empowered to bring into action what they cared about. What was different in her story from the many others that I had heard until then was that she acted upon her calling by founding Syinc. Syinc, further gave ample opportunities to other youth to shine and experience community action. Bernise realize that that which is moulded could be un-moulded and re-shaped.

I participated in my first Design-Thinking workshop with many other passionate and compassionate youth, who wanted to make a difference to the society. The field was created. Syinc, in Singapore, is a part design studio, part civic organisation, part innovation lab which works with like-minded partners to find creative solutions for social impact. Shaun Koh, the steward gardener has gems that youth can learn from.

Similarly, I met Sailesh Mishra, from Mumbai, another fine day. He has a calling to work for the elderly and founded Silver Inning Foundation. While Singapore was campaigning on 'active ageing' in a positive way, I was following Sailesh's work virtually, and noticing how the impassioned leaders ask similar fundamental questions, even if they come from different cultures. So much for cultural difference, when it comes to the quintessence of life!

Sailesh and his team advocate for an elderly-friendly world, where ageing becomes a positive and rewarding experience.

Talking to many other people who have volunteered in either of these two organisations, or many other changemakers, it became clear how people are keen to learn from the mistakes of the past. The past could be their personal past, or a historical one with evidence of wars, genocide and violence at a global level. It is important for your generation to remember the mistakes made in history by other generations. Again, in my times, we are witnessing local and global revolutions because of the ease of accessing information and spreading stories for awareness in an instant. Many people who wish to be part of something bigger, wish to contribute and to learn are finding opportunities on a large scale.

Social capital is the new essential quintessence. It is a just a matter of finding 'your people' based on the direction you wish to explore, locally or globally.

The question I still hold is even as we get together for a cause, are we willing to work individually on ourselves to refine not only the mind space with knowledge and information, but also the heart space with values and practices to refine our skills of being together as humanity for humanity?

I am afraid that most communities end up debating with each other and fighting for resources and hence beyond civil and world wars, I have seen major mini community cold wars. The principles at work are similar as those of identity, separation and segregation. Intergenerational and multi cultural truths go missing due to lack of conversations and co-learning.

Learning communities is a possibility.
Elders and youth mentoring each other and learning from each other is a possibility.

Safe and strengths-based spaces that contribute to societal impact is a possibility.

Developing a germ of an idea into action that enables others is a possibility.

It all depends on what are you looking for and asking of yourself and others.

It all begins from the inner world of sense making of your own experiences, both the good and the bad ones.
Learning is possible from the past to change the future.

Are you ready to sign up, irrespective of your age, gender, class, caste or any other distinction that has felt disempowering so far, for a thriving community of the future?

Such communities exist. They ask quality questions in a way that tastefully invites others to be curious, to seek the answers together, multi-culturally and multi-generationally. Certain communities birthed practices and methodologies and platforms that attended to the engagement of its members' collective intelligence and knowing to be informed of various aspects pertaining to any topic. Some such communities that are nurturing some key methodologies that I see thriving in my times in both physical and virtual, local and global spaces are Story-telling circles, Theatre circles, Coaching circles, World Café, Open Space, Pro Action Café, Appreciative Inquiry, Design Thinking, TED and its various TEDx events, co-working spaces as the Hub, Presencing Institute etcetra.

I am still learning.
We are still learning.

And yet, in your times, some of this learning will serve and some will become irrelevant. So, I hope and pray that you have a germ of an idea of what you want and start from there to explore, collaborate and live. Practice questioning, listening, learning and enjoying the quintessence of life. I trust you to practice the practices that uplift your Qi, exercise questions to keep your spirit awake and build quality relations with your self and others, along your way.

Quidditch magic wishes,

Grandma

PS: So, my lovely grandchildren, what are your stories of being in your quintessence of life as your *Practice of Satsang*, in your times?

*"Forget yourself for others and others will never forget you,
as told to me by my mother in my childhood."*

-Sailesh Mishra (2014)
-(Change Maker, Founder & President
at Silver Inning Foundation,
Mumbai, India)

Now, it is time for Practice.
You may create your own or experiment with one I suggest below.

Practice
(Q)

To reflect.

- Pick any one incident from your personal life that has left a mark.
- Ask questions that give you diverse perspectives on the same incident.
  Example-
  o What aspect of you did that incident draw? Would you be different?
  o What is the relevance of that incident in the bigger schema of life?
  o What is the impact of that incident on your loved ones and on others?
  o What is the first powerful step you can take towards peace?
- The action could be that of love, forgiveness, learning, deepening a value
  and that of integrity in your inner world. It could also be a first step to
  help another in the other world.

PS: A person becomes wiser through reflection and constructive action at any
given age and phase of life.

Revering the Art of Hosting ~

~ Letters to my grandchildren ~

My dear little ones, out of the many words you will learn starting with the alphabet 'R', I have a few fundamental ones to share. In addition to 'Rat' or 'Rail', words that helped me to understand the world, the outer world, I was curious to gain access to the mysterious inner world that exists within us. The secret to peace, happiness and fulfillment lies in there. Our inner world determines how we respond to the outer world - people, places and perspectives. Practicing the essence of the few fundamental words below has been life-giving, nourishing and key to expanding possibilities for me

As you grow each day into beautiful beings, I invite you to experiment, play and discover the essence of these words in your life. As you master the game, you will get clues to master your life and create your own future that is meaningful, day-by-day. The key is to choose wisely and practice consciously. Remember, whatever you practice; consciously, sub-consciously, or unconsciously, right or wrong, it grows stronger. So, what do you choose?

R for 'Remembrance'

- What is your inner knowing and remembering of your unity with nature?
- What do you practice to allow stillness in your life?

R for 'Reasoning'

- How do you know what you know?
- What are new ways of knowing that you are integrating in your life? What gifts does this bring to your life and your relationships?

R for 'Radiance'

- Do you recognize the radiance your acceptance brings on others' faces and souls?
- What service brings you radiant joy, peace and love?

Other words, still starting with 'R', also served me but only for short-term. Practice of the essence of these words fed my ego and exhausted me in the long-term as I found them to be life-depleting;

R for 'Rude', 'Ruthless' and 'Robotlike'.

Practice of *Satsang* with Community – A Story

Revering the Art of Hosting ~

Where or what is 'home' to you?

Do you remember the first time you played host to family, or friends?

Who is your community to which you belong? How do they host you?

I think I first hosted my favourite cloth doll from Nepal (the one I had mentioned in the story of Journeys with Meaning that was almost ceased by Check Point officers at the Nepal border, close to my home. I had learnt not so much in words but as an experience that when you care enough about something, you take the first step towards its well-being.) I would make sure that 'Shanky' (the doll) was well fed and kept warm. Since childhood, even though I was not allowed to have any *chai*, I would host a 'tea-party' at home. Grandmother taught me how to make invisible *'chai'* and I served it to all my dolls in small steel toy cups, with invisible biscuits in small steel toy plates. I gave one to *nanima* too. I learnt well when I observed the adults host guests. It seemed apt that my dolls were guests in a phase in my life as they soon left, and I began to help host real people at home. Except, real people are not dolls!

Interestingly, as I began to host real guests, along with *nanima*, I realized that there are two levels of hosting. The first one is the physical level of hosting; get the guests seated comfortably, disappear in the kitchen, play with the decoration of cutlery, tea and snacks and offer it elegantly (without dropping it – well done!). I would get confused with the second level of hosting. It is like the mental level where the thoughts are not visible. So I would take the words audible to me, literally. So for example, if one said that one is not hungry and does not want the snacks, I would promptly remove the food, or not even offer it in the first place (which is considered rude in my culture.) I would not understand why couldn't people just say what they want or mean what they say! *Nanima* would scowl at my very reasonable questions and taught me the discreet ways of the second level of hosting.

It was at mini-costs that I learnt to be discreet. For example, it is ok for guests to come to your home unannounced even if you do not like but it is not ok for you to let them know the truth! I wanted to tell them to call before visiting but I was told that I would inconvenience them. The prayers that I was learning in the convent school made sense, 'grant that I shall never seek … to be understood as to understand…' the practice was so difficult. I would often think that dolls and imaginary friends are so much better. I do not have to pretend with them.

I wanted to stick to the physical hosting as that is much easier and leave the mental hosting to grandmother, who preferred the other way round! She was probably scared that I would burn the kitchen down, or so I would think. I was afraid of burning a relationship down! Yet, I acquiesced. She had a valid point that sometimes she would be unable to hear despite the hearing aid and comprehend what the other was saying. So, like it or not, I had to grow up.

Hosting differs in communities based on some invisible ground rules. I wondered who created those ground rules and if there were Check Point officers to cease the rules that do not serve!

Soon enough, I always *knew* it that conversations have to be hosted lest they should go awry. Reminding people about deep listening, inviting them to speak mindfully and truthfully and creating the space for exploration were some of the ground rules or principles that we had learnt as hosts in the methodology of Pro-Action café. I had found it interesting when I had first heard of the term 'host' officially.

It had made sense to host a group of people in conversations. It also helps to remind the people to access their own host-selves. They tend to shift away from their roles and positions to treat every idea, perspective and belief as a guest. Rumi's poem, 'The Guest' is one of my favourite pieces to put in the center for everyone to consider. It helps manage the inner child in adults leaning towards the option of terrifying tantrums when they perceive their metaphorical favourite doll (perspective, idea, thought, belief) to be under threat of being ceased by the other.

Once I grew up more, I connected the dots between hosting conversations, hosting silence and hosting relationships. Guess, we do not need Check Point officers with ground rules in a community as much as compassionate beings who help you to belong. I knew in my guts that there is a third level of hosting although I did not know what that might be.

I was curious about compassionate beings in our communities. I saw some light and a lot of darkness. I saw and felt a lot of alienation, emptiness, individualism, loneliness and the feeling of being lost amongst people. Hosting guests felt like a chore for many as one tries to show their best sides, which is interpreted as the richest, materialistic face for fear that, people may think less of the person otherwise. The individual soul and person when forgotten behind the blink-blink of riches or perceptions creates a wide, yawning, ugly gap. The worst is when this truth is not even acknowledged.

Many individuals are afraid and hence put up their defenses for fear of being attacked, being enthusiastically fixed up as a problem, or left feeling lesser of themselves based on the views of the other. Many are aware that they are putting up defenses and many are also unaware. Thinking terribly of themselves, they already assume that the other will think the same or worse of them. As such, they meet and host with a steel armour, hiding behind it, ready to attack, if attacked and end up leaving the ones they are hosting feeling small. It is because they themselves feel small in the first place.

Eureka!

I surmised that the reason why the second kind of mental hosting is difficult and is not enough is not because of the guests but because of me. If I am in a worthy space, which people can trust, then they will not act difficult. But if I am a doubtful space, which is untrustworthy, then people are afraid to be vulnerable, to show up as to who they truly are and hide behind hollow stories of politeness even though their hearts may yearn for depth of truth. I soon learnt that worth is not created by material wealth but an abundance of inner wealth.

It is that simple. If only each individual took up the responsibility for the spaces they are as human beings; cluttered in their own opinions or clear and invitational for another!

The mental level of hosting can be fun too when it is transparent. It is meaningful when safety is created in a community of acceptance, of belongingness, of care and compassion for all members and guests, irrespective of one's wealth, status and achievements. Different strokes for different folks! Acceptance, belongingness and care can be demonstrated and accepted in many different forms. For some, the premise of the strong abstract container could be spiritual. For others, it was environment and an eco-village. For many more, it became interest groups that opened up to attend to the whole of the person.

In my curious search, I stumbled across the Art of Hosting website.

I knew it! I knew that there is an art to hosting. It was a moment of significant discovery to find like-minded, diverse people who chose to come together as practitioners under the umbrella of the Art of Hosting; thriving global communities keen to create social, economic and political impact through hosting!

One of the first things that struck me was the active online global community that shared with gusto their discoveries from their local communities. They shared their fears, their doubts, their questions, their personal styles, and their assumptions in a circle and space of respect. It attracted many individuals and the circle expanded as more and more people across countries wished to step in to unlearn, to learn and to contribute. The Art of Hosting, stewarded by generous warrior and nurturer souls, who care about the truth from diverse parts of the field, wields many participative methodologies that allow a beginner like me to learn and apply. The methodologies balance between ancient wisdom and relevant realities in the field, today.

So, while I was wondering what was the third level of hosting, I learnt about the four-fold practice of hosting. I wish that they had taught me this in school.

The four-fold practice of hosting, symbolically representing ancient wisdom to dance with the truth of the current, unfolding times surprised me, touched me, mesmerized me. It held a component that I never deemed as important, and later on, when more and more friends and fellow travelers learnt, some were equally surprised. I readily became a practitioner and underwent the following transformation in my hosting.

The first practice is 'Hosting Yourself'. The principles are simple, to take care of oneself, mind, body and soul.

How come I never heard of this in my community (by this I mean the one I was born in to) as I was growing up? The self was taught to be put at last for fear of turning selfish. But, ancient wisdom in my community did put the core of the self first! 'Namaste' means 'the divine in me bows to the divine in you'. Then when did people forget about the divine in themselves and others? Little wonder, if they do not recognize the divine in themselves, they cannot recognize it in the other. For whatever reason, when self care is confused with selfishness, when one is taught to be present to others but absent to the self's needs, the balance is lost and the hosting is not sustainable. What a beautiful reminder to host oneself with acceptance, care and compassion and feel that you belong in your own body.

Even as I was reminded of that, I remembered all the pain moments in my community, when I was ridiculed because I was short and diminutive and wore spectacles as a little child. Family members, maybe because they were not mindful or because they did not know any better, would make me stand next to their children to compare heights! Soon, I saw that I was not the only one. Other children were compared with others who were fat! Yet, others were compared with others who were dark, and dumb, and ugly, and spoke funnily, and were clumsy and naughty and so on. Perhaps the adults then did not know about the violence they inflicted on the inner minds of the children. Perhaps the adults then had been subject to similar violence in their childhood. So, 'Hosting Yourself' meant cleansing oneself of the past conditioning that does not serve and loving oneself despite the limitations that advertisements, markets and some people promote for their selfish gains. The day I accepted my short height as a gift and as something that I could not change past teenage years, I felt a sense of freedom unparalleled that helped me host any conversations around height and looks later. What an empowering gift to accept oneself in a way that enables self to empower others too.

The second practice is 'Being Hosted'. The principles are to allow yourself to be hosted, to be humble and to trust.

This seemed stranger to me than the first practice! I could not draw a parallel with anything explicit from my culture but then remembered how father would always speak of the principles of giving and receiving to balance and build meaningful relationships. The more I spoke to people from diverse cultures, the more I realized how people were afraid to trust and allow themselves to be hosted. It became easier to be independent. Café cultures, restaurant cultures emerged in many markets and hosting shifted from homes to hotels and bars. That took care of the first kind of hosting as I defined it, simplistically in physical terms. Yet, what about the mental or emotional kind of hosting?

I read about how coaching and other helping professions emerged as society felt estranged, empty and helpless, with the lack of conversations that feed the soul. Even as family or friends, many were ready to be there for each other but afraid to ask for help and were shy of being a burden or a bother. Some of my friends and I spoke of perhaps that might have been the cause of the misinterpretation of independence with selfishness as the signals one got was to fend for oneself. It went against the law of nature, as we were all inter-dependent, irrespective of what we chose to believe. Many in the Art of Hosting circles spoke of the peace and freedom they felt when they realized that they were in a community that looked after the whole. One could finally think of beyond oneself. Stories of being hosted and the courage it takes to trust began to thrive. Practising small steps with my friends of offering what I could (which was definitely not culinary skills) and requesting for kitchen help soon became a joyful space of creating trust. We practiced hosting ourselves and being hosted with abundance in food for thought, food for soul and food for the body.

The third practice is 'Hosting Others'. The principles are that of initiation to step up to host others, to collaborate and to care.

I dare say, my Barbie dolls, Nepalese doll and toys had taught me well about caring because they would deteriorate if I did not. I had learnt about fragility of human bonds through many stories and examples since childhood. This third principle seemed familiar and intuitive to me. I was surprised then to see that it was not the same with everyone else. The reasons could be attributed to shyness, to lack of exposure and experience in hosting diversity or complexity as some perceived it to be, to lack of time and energy etc for many people. I began to explore the lens of scarcity vis-à-vis abundance that determines the willingness to step up to host others. Stories abound of how many travelers are hosted across the globe by communities in villages who do not have much to offer, yet they offer what they can, be it a square meal or necessity but with a lot of love.

Rich stories abound in couch-surfing communities, inter-religious and spiritual communities, and even in local and global communities of people hosting others, enabling others and supporting others. The shift in the expansion of the circle is felt visibly when 'Others' becomes a subjective term as people begin to belong and feel as one community. Scientists and mystics sit in conversations around their perceptions of one-ness, intuition, love and care. That is when I understood the Art of Hosting and the Science of Hosting and the vast universe of wisdom to be gained through knowledge, through experiences, through observation and through hosting.

The fourth practice is 'To Co-create'. The principles are to host the collective wisdom from the individuals and the whole.

At a primitive part of my being, I felt great resonance with this four-fold practice. This lens helped me re-look at my communities and spaces and I began to see gifts of co-creation in small and big ways in joint-families, amongst friends, at workplaces and in diverse interests. In many cultures, the elders attend to the process and the intention. Broken stories emerge from some families and communities when for whatever reasons, the elders could not attend to the rising complexities. Inspiring stories balanced those of how elders invited the youngsters to co-create with them, to help understand and act accordingly.

Art of Hosting is an organic, global community that emerged as such. No one person leads or controls this group. Rather, it is a group of stewards, hosts, apprentices and learners who come together in many small and big circles across the globe to learn, to practice, to apply processes and methods that enable more and more people to participate and to co-create in their own contexts. Each of the methodologies have an interesting birthing story too and how those communities have chiseled and co-created the method in practice to serve more and more communities.

I met Toke Paludan Moller, one of the co-creators and pioneering steward of this Art of Hosting practice, space and consciousness, whose questions, messages and stories made me host my thoughts, emotions and dreams. It was interesting as through my lenses and background, I immediately likened him to a grandfather status (never asking him if he liked that or not!) That would make him your great-great-Danish-grandfather! I likened his grit and determination with *nanaji*. Although his practice of hosting relationships and conversations helped me see the articulation that I always willed from *nanaji*.

Toke called himself a student in the *dojo* (Japanese term for school) of life. I saw him pro-actively co-create spaces and build strong containers with other stewards, participants and hosts from the world. The containers allowed for feisty philosophies and personalities, complex challenges and opportunities and lightness and resolve for action to dance in it. People from across the world come to these spaces; government, multi-nationals, non-government organisations, businesses, entrepreneurs, students, artists, home-makers. It is hosted to host other present or future hosts and practitioners of mindfulness. I met many a superhero in that space. Principled women and men, who role-modeled a way of being that was only imaginary in my limited experience.

Participating in this community, I often felt hosting processes and groups and conversations was a dance much like the dance of Siva, the Hindu deity, that destroys conceptions and perceptions and ego that do not serve and allows for creativity and co-creation to emerge that will serve our and future generations.

I realized my good intentions and bad habits as I began to practice. One of the rules is to never practice alone. Values imperceptibly form the foundations of the Art of Hosting. Toke admonished and brought to the awareness the subtle differences between co-creation through invitation, patience and collaboration versus pretentious co-creation through force, haste and contention. He empathized with me and spoke of consciousness. For years, serving in the industry of events management, he knew in his gut that the potential was untapped with the number of resources invested to bring people together. With his mates, he explored the truth of the discontent. Gradually, the Art of Hosting as an invitation emerged, which is going viral in my times. It is what more and more people are yearning for as they host their truths to realize that what matters is peace and love. Something is shifting. Are we aware and hosting it?

How can we bring peace, love, collaboration and caring in workplaces and communities? The Art of Hosting practitioners, much like a giant beehive, are practising to produce honey for future generations and ours.

The key is to practice. Repetitive practice, process consciousness that were not part of my over-achievement, result-oriented drive emerged as some other old patterns began to die. It felt like a re-birth. I was not alone in my struggle and discovery. Finally, here was a space where I could trust strangers to host me despite of my doubts, fears and limitations. Conversations on leadership, on change, on life and death emerged in explorations, in perspectives where each was listened to and given the space to share her or his own truth. I identified with the spirit of *Satsang*.

Practice of *Satsang* with community is possible for economic, political and social problems, in a non-religious manner. It is aiming for peaceful sacredness for life.

I hope and pray for you that you discover the art of hosting your inner wholistic world. I trust you to practice the art of honouring the different forms of reasoning, remembrance that comes from the same radiance of yourself and others.

Really love you,

Grandma.

PS: So, my lovely grandchildren, what are your stories of your art of hosting as your *Practice of Satsang,* in your times?

"Art of Hosting is rooted in ancient practices of getting together as authentic human beings and talking about what matters. We just have to remember that and practice.

One is born with the gift of hosting. Art, because it implies that no one is an expert.

It is an evolving practice with deep understanding of the transformative power of listening to yourself and others and gauging what matters. Through conversations and progressive education, societies have come out of despair.

The skills, methodologies, architecture allow people who would otherwise not be able to talk to come together with an attitude to not give up on the possibility that we can find solutions in societies, organisations, families despite the differences.

It all starts with a willingness and intention to shift something.

The four-fold practice helps bring intention to action. It is based on the world-view that everything is connected.

So, what is the purpose and intention behind the conversation?

How can it serve the grandchildren and the planet?"

-Toke Paludan Moller (2014)
(CEO and Host of learning
and practicing humanity at
InterChange for our world,
Steward Art of Hosting)

Now, it is time for Practice.
You may create your own or experiment with one I suggest below.

Practice
(R)

To be aware of your own comfort or discomfort in hosting. Notice your stories of -

- Hosting Yourself – What is your understanding of your own needs, paradoxical as they may seem?
- Being Hosted – Try trusting someone you normally would not and discover your learning about forgiveness and fun from the experience.
- Hosting Others – What is your comfort zone and practice to be sustainable?
- Co-create – Test your patterns of creativity and partner with someone different to discover anew.

PS: What communities or concepts are you nurturing in practice and consciousness?

Social entrepreneurship, hey AIESEC!

~ Letters to my grandchildren ~

My dear little ones, out of the many words you will learn starting with the alphabet 'S', I have a few fundamental ones to share. In addition to 'Sheep' or 'Ship', words that helped me to understand the world, the outer world, I was curious to gain access to the mysterious inner world that exists within us. The secret to peace, happiness and fulfillment lies in there. Our inner world determines how we respond to the outer world - people, places and perspectives. Practicing the essence of the few fundamental words below has been life-giving, nourishing and key to expanding possibilities for me

As you grow each day into beautiful beings, I invite you to experiment, play and discover the essence of these words in your life. As you master the game, you will get clues to master your life and create your own future that is meaningful, day-by-day. The key is to choose wisely and practice consciously. Remember, whatever you practice; consciously, sub-consciously, or unconsciously, right or wrong, it grows stronger. So, what do you choose?

S for 'Stillness'

- What is your relationship with silence, solitude and stillness?
- What do you practice to invite stillness and its wisdom in your life?

S for 'Simplicity'

- How do you value simplicity?
- What are the lenses you hold to generate simplicity and meaning in uncertain times for yourself and others?

S for 'Supportive'

- What is your philosophy and action to extend support to others who may or may not ask you for help?
- How comfortable are you to accept support graciously, maybe even seek it?

Other words, still starting with 'S', also served me but only for short-term. Practice of the essence of these words fed my ego and exhausted me in the long-term as I found them to be life-depleting;

S for 'Sarcastic', 'Stingy' and 'Stereotyping'.

Practice of *Satsang* with Community – A Story

Social entrepreneurship, hey AIESEC!

Youth is defined diversely in different countries and the age attributed ranges upto 35 years in some places. I just saw a banner that says, 'Keep calm – 40 is the new 20' and had a light laugh with a friend celebrating her 40s and wondering what is the 30s, and 20s then! Feeling young, and perhaps that is most crucial, the attitude more than age, she described her dreams ahead and of continuing the difference she made in her community.

The sacredness of youth – it is a time in many people's lives of exploration, discovery, having fun, making mistakes, laughing even while falling and believing in possibilities, daring and living. Little wonder that one wishes to feel young eternally.

Which communities celebrate and respect the treasures that youth brings and creates resources and opportunities for its members to grow and to learn?

The first community that I belong to is the one by virtue of being born in it. I was curious about it too and did my research on premises of educational choices made by the community for the younger generation. Born in a business-community, not shy of traveling, where the role of women were defined in a certain way, I did not feel a sense of belonging and trust in the community. Would my community understand if I shared my thoughts? Would they even listen to my interpretation of shared values and thereby, choices I make? Would they tell me that the individual, or worse, in my times, opinions of a girl, does not matter in front of the numbers and hence I should/ought to/must follow the norms? Were it not for my parent's protection and blessings, would the community allow me to experiment in my education and in life and be my parent's strength if I failed?

I had my doubts as soon rumours spread about me in a certain segment of distant relatives that the only way I could survive in Singapore is because I was secretly married! Secretly!!! And why 'the only way' – is it because I am a woman?

Even though I believed in celebrating the truth of who I am, it showed me who wished to celebrate with me, who had enough curiosity to know of the truth at least even if one does not join in the celebrations and who did not care about my truth.

My inner mind erupted as a volcano and I reacted strongly when I heard that. My deepest fear was manifested that if I make one wrong step, the community/ larger family would pounce on my parents who had made their child's choice, their choice! Despite doing well and working very hard, my parents and I were subject to ridicule. When I asked mother to confront the relative, she calmly asked me if the rumour was true. I was taken aback by this childish question. "Well then, why must we feed what is not true and waste our energy? People will believe what they want to believe. You cannot control their beliefs but you can direct your energy well!" my mother responded in a grounded way. My bruised ego retreated as I was comforted by my parent's wisdom.

Little wonder I have friends who do not wish to be part of any community. I was angry and spent a part of my time generalizing about the futility of communities. Then I met more friends who helped expand my consciousness. Some belonged to and felt very gratified as part of spiritual groups where they could nurture their wholistic selves. Some shared about their identity struggles and how joining LGBT groups gave them a ground that was whisked under from them un-caringly by communities they might have been born into. Yet, others spoke of communities for social service, business development, sustainability and so forth. I learnt to let go of judgment and wondered where to focus my energy? I soon realized the possibilities of a global community. Guess our human species is tuned to hunger for the community feeling, perhaps for surviving.

A thriving community is one where multi-generational learning takes places and where people care enough for each other, even if they are strangers, to include and involve each other in the workings that serve the community back, making it stickier, stronger and safer, I believe.

Speaking of communities with friends, most of us identified with AIESEC as each of our respective cultural communities in which we were born, posed socio-cultural challenges. AIESEC is youth organized, youth led and one that I believe, as my experiential truth, brings out the quintessence of youth.

It has a multi-generational component as we have an AIESEC Alumni, and stewards who check in, mentor and co-create opportunities with and for the youth. However, it is one of the well-known international organisations that allow youth to create and manage its own experiences and business, lead and follow, succeed and fail. There are other youth communities too. Invite you to research and join one to experience a community feeling directly.

Often in life, one misses a treasure when it is gone. Gathering as AIESEC alumni after a few years, we had a lovely evening sharing stories from our youthful lives that enabled us, supported us and helped us in our jobs and choices later on. Some reminisced of the challenges in joining the AIESEC group, traveling across miles and cities as their universities in their countries may not have offered the opportunity. Others fondly remembered the opportunities presented to them, which were beyond their wildest dreams, the friendships they nurtured and the cross-cultural exposure from which they learnt much. A year for an AIESEC youth was starkly different from the common youth in terms of exposure and experience. AIESEC days were full of creating, practicing, attending conferences, organizing events with the intention of creating socio-cultural impact, traveling for internships and returning home with treasures in forms of learning and relationships and more.

Needless to say, once they joined their full-time jobs, a void appeared as many realized the quality of work given to them as young officers were worse off than what AIESEC co-created for internships with many well-meaning partners and organisations. Also, with a mindset to create their own lives and building opportunities step-by-step, in a real job, one was confounded by the ways things worked where by virtue of being junior, one was hardly engaged to create the path for the visions and missions that organisations espouse for.

Without any major survey, one could count the essentials and values by which the youth self-organised themselves in AIESEC where one is not even paid and yet, does not mind working into late hours. Thousands of youth beat to a similar heart beat across the globe in different chapters and co-create their dream projects, dream events and dream teams.

Once into a cushy job, which is also the realization of a dream, one wonders how to sustain learning, and a spirit of community and friendship. Some want to continue in their jobs but begin to miss a sense of purpose that they felt where they knew that they were part of something bigger, something meaningful and something kind. Some wonder how and when to contribute to the social sector.

Torn asunder by such questions, we witnessed few of the AIESEC community members quit their well-paying, corporate jobs and enter the field of social entrepreneurship so that they could continue to dedicate their youth precious days in service of creating spaces that would truly make a positive impact.

Your Chinese grandfather, Peter was part of AIESEC at a time when it was starting small, there. 10 years later, he returned to his local chapter to share about his social entrepreneurship. One of the first things he shared on his return was not about the colossal cheer he received for the unique path he had taken but about the pride he felt as China's AIESEC had grown 10 times in the last 10 years! He inspired the youth there helping them see 10 years into the future and reminding them about quality work and relationships than quantity work and transactional meetings.

Peter Yang created Empact, a one-stop shared service provider dedicated to the non-profit and social enterprise communities. He developed the idea with his team and soon helped hundreds of non-profit organisations to benefit and upscale their productivity with the help of quality volunteers who offered their strengths that they used anyways in their own jobs. Co-creating win-win stories, Peter and his team started a spiral up ward strengths-based movement and a feeling of community where one enabled the other to grow. He made me believe in humanity as at a stage in my life, I was surrounded by examples of inhumane, and crab-like behaviours of people pulling people down!

What made him resilient, responsible and revere his own germ of an idea dream towards a bigger cause? One has to meet him to know a fulfilling answer to that! He describes his turning point in his inner world when he realized that his life purpose was much bigger thank his career or making a living alone. I learnt from him the no-easy-way-out-method of working on one-self and being truthful to oneself. He was a part of other communities as Landmark and Power of Now, where he actively pursued developing his awareness and being to serve better.

He took a working space in the HUB Singapore, which is another example of a community built with purpose. Grace Sai, co-founder and CEO of HUB, had worked incessantly on this dream of hers to bring HUB to Singapore and create a physical space for people from diverse walks of life to work and interact with. We had hosted Pro-action café there and over time, witnessed its Indra net growing.

Curious in heart, when I visited the HUB, I met many friends. One amongst them was another social entrepreneur, Ashwin Subramaniam, whom I had met as an AIESEC member long time ago. He was studying in college and even then I was struck by his practices of meditation and inquiry through reading Ramakrishna, Buddhism and much more. I recall one Saturday morning when he invited me to join him for meditation and visit to one of the Buddhist temples in Singapore. It was a peaceful morning, where I did not know of the workings of his ideas (perhaps he did not either) that may have wondered 'how to bring about peace on a larger scale?'

He defined his work around stories of adventure that inspire social impact, 'Gone Adventurin'. Ashwin continued to nurture the purpose to strengthen a community keen to undertake adventures and connect with the larger community in developing countries where sustaining basic life itself can be a big adventure. Creating holidays with purpose for people who are keen on adventure, he works with his team to have those adventures in the regions, which can be benefited not only by the finance, but also by their presence.

I recall his story from attending the celebration of his pioneering creation, 'Gone Cyclin', co-founded then with Yasmine Khater. The challenge was to cycle/bike across East Timor to raise funds to contribute to the economy there. Ashwin had sought help for initial funding and was turned down many times. Yet, his key learning was not to give up. His path had begun with many challenges, illuminating the entire path that was to unfold, over the years. He persevered and finally found like-minded fellow-travelers and friends who joined up for the adventure. Thus, began 'Gone Cyclin'.

Suddenly, weekends for the cohort who had signed up became enmeshed with cycles, helmets, maps. Stretching their limits, preparing for the big race, they took it up as a discipline and were rewarded in the deepest sense by their visit to East Timor. Not only did they complete the challenge, but also met their intention of raising around S$30,000, which was all given away as donations to the local communities and organisations there. Visiting the villages, interacting with the locals, they returned to the global city of Singapore with teeming muscles and beaming hearts. It was one of the most meaningful trips for both the designers and the join - ups and an inspiration for other friends like us, who listened to their visceral stories of individual experiences, collective experiences, ephemeral memories and eternal insights.

More and more friends joined his adventures and were soon drawn into the circle of real adventure of life.

Another common friend from AIESEC, Terrence Seah, who was born and brought up in the classic way of Singapore, had signed up for the adventure of cycling in Cambodia. Tasked to monitor a particular path, he realized after a while that most cyclists seem to have bypassed that path. He found himself alone, lost, without a phone or money in the middle of almost-no-where. Trusting that the search team would come up for him, he spent another couple of hours playing with the children, teaching them basic English words while keeping an eye out for signs.

As the day began to progress, he bid those children bye and began to cycle, asking folks on the way for direction. Bereft of his own basic comforts of atleast a phone, some money and hence, food or water, he realized how might it be to spend a day with no money, food or water! He was no longer only literally lost.

Something deep had begun to stir within as he grappled with his inner and outer worlds right then. Cycling along, still lost, he began to see with new eyes the meaning behind basic living in Singapore. This meant the availability of an Iphone, couple of dollars to buy food from the many Kopitiams (local cafes) in almost every nook and corner, freely available drinkable water, well-construed city with the world's best transportation system, maps and directions,...... family,..... friends,.....the list is long. It is abundant.

Standing on some cross-roads in Cambodia, he ironically saw himself in the cross-roads of his life, where all the decisions he took and inadvertently chose would create an irreversible impact. He noticed not only 'new eyes' for himself, but also a 'new voice' – his own voice in his head, (or was it the heart!) asking, what is his purpose of life? What does basic, conscious living really mean? What are some changes he would like to make, looking ahead? With little to nil distraction from people, places, phones and the other gadgets that demand our attention, he spent hour after hour cycling in the questions that began to emerge. Perspectives that seem to be hiding in some far-away land purposefully strode smilingly to meet the lone, lost traveler.

Riding on, he did something that was rare for him. He took a deep breath, felt grateful for the experience, even though he was not home yet and suddenly trusted himself. He acknowledged his intuition, and with this new awareness, synchronistically found himself at a juncture to see two members of the team far down the road, who were stuck with their bikes. Call it good luck, chance or perhaps one can find logic in there, he met them, and found his way to safety and home before it grew too dark.

All in a day's work, he returned from that adventure triumphant of opening the door that had stood jammed for years in his life. With further introspection, action and inspiration, he slowly and surely made the desired basic changes in his life to live in a fulfilling way. He stepped up to join the AIESEC Alumni leadership, amidst the busyness of life, to continue to nurture the community he loved, create more opportunities – to be lost and found.

The circle of community consciousness and co-creation continues.

I hope and pray for you that you do not waste your youth days but stay curious to find the entrepreneur in you who has a positive impact on others. It may or may not be in the business form, but in a form that attends to life and meaning. I trust you to practice stillness, support others and enjoy the simplicity and sacredness of your spirit as you build relations with your self and others, along your way.

Simply yours,

Grandma

P.S. So, my lovely grandchildren, what are your stories of being and belonging in a community of choice as your *Practice of Satsang*, in your times?

"Live your life as a contribution and make your youth count."

-Peter Yang (2014)
-(Change Maker, Founder – Empact)

Now, it is time for Practice.
You may create your own or experiment with one I suggest below.

Practice
(S)

To enjoy sacredness in every-day ordinary moments of life.

- Invite intentional sacredness in your every-day moments of life.
- Notice in what forms or formlessness sacredness shows up for you.
- Enjoy stillness amidst the busyness to listen to the voice of your soul
- Be guided for all aspects of your life.

PS: Notice how ordinary moments turn into extra-ordinary.

Things to Think about ~

~ Letters to my grandchildren ~

My dear little ones, out of the many words you will learn starting with the alphabet 'T', I have a few fundamental ones to share. In addition to 'Tomato' or 'Tree', words that helped me to understand the world, the outer world, I was curious to gain access to the mysterious inner world that exists within us. The secret to peace, happiness and fulfillment lies in there. Our inner world determines how we respond to the outer world - people, places and perspectives. Practicing the essence of the few fundamental words below has been life-giving, nourishing and key to expanding possibilities for me

As you grow each day into beautiful beings, I invite you to experiment, play and discover the essence of these words in your life. As you master the game, you will get clues to master your life and create your own future that is meaningful, day-by-day. The key is to choose wisely and practice consciously. Remember, whatever you practice; consciously, sub-consciously, or unconsciously, right or wrong, it grows stronger. So, what do you choose?

T for 'Trust'

- What is your relationship with trusting yourself?
- Who are you so others can trust you?

T for 'Truth'

- How curious are you about the truth?
- To what lengths are you willing to seek your truth, even if it means disappointing others?

T for 'Transformational'

- What is the form you are willing to let go of and take?
- What is your moment-to-moment awareness and practice of *satsang*?

Other words, still starting with 'T', also served me but only for short-term. Practice of the essence of these words fed my ego and exhausted me in the long-term as I found them to be life-depleting;

T for 'Timid', 'Tricky' and 'Tempted'.

Practice of *Satsang* with Community
– A Tail of Thoughts

Things to Think about ~

What would be the tale of our lives that we will share with the future generations?

What will be the tale of your lives that you will share with our future generations?

What will be their tale?

All these tales would have something in common too-transformational and transmutational moments in human history and tales of conscious living and practice of *satsang* in diverse forms and new norms.

When everything changes, what remains?

What is left behind?

What is left behind is what has been there since the beginning of this process-truth, consciousness and bliss that is evolving – or wait, is it that it just is and that my understanding and appreciation of it is evolving? I do not know, yet.

In this game of time and space and timelessness, taking a full 360 turn, what is your anchor that you offer to family, friends, fellow-travelers, colleagues, clients, community? It is the priceless resource, which is YOU!

Nothing and nobody can replace you.

The truth of the 'you' is that it has the magical capacity to change and transform. Guess, who knows the secret magical incantation? You!

Your truth may show up in sounds, colours, questions, stories, or alphabets!

Why have I chosen to play with alphabets as I write from my heart to you?

It has been my truth to make sense of this world in this way.

It was my anchor when I first spoke in English with *nanima*. I pointed at this and she pointed at that. She taught me their names in English that brought much joy between us, and my first conscious experience of learning, or what I can recall. I would hold her nose and scream, 'nose'! It would turn slightly pink and I would laugh at that.

We had word games between us, word plays and before I knew it, I was teaching her English when she lamented that she had not been allowed to complete her studies. That is when I realized the experience of a process, of impermanence and of not taking things personally. After all, all our relationships are but roles that we play and it is possible to make the exchanges amidst those roles interesting.

What if we learn from as much as we teach the younger generation?

What if we learn from our own tales?

The thing is I bet we all do that.

The thing is, despite that, I have seen people get stuck in their own tales, chasing their own tails. That is when we need the other.

The thing is, the other could be a family member, friend, fellow traveler, colleague, client, community member or even a community's guidelines.

The thing is, the other could also be a different aspect of you that you has not been tapped into for various reasons. Sometimes, courage, willingness, openness, trust and love lie hidden in our beings if we have not practiced them, enough.

The thing is, we have so much of information, facts, knowledge to satisfy our rationale selves in our age and time, and yet we struggle to be wise. We struggle with irrational fear, emotions, dreams, and desires that stop us from putting into practice all that we know of. And then when we do not put into practice, we do not truly know.

The thing is, we forget that this consistent inconsistency is part of being human – for a human being.

The thing is, the whole self emerges when we study the subject we are interested in, practice it despite successes or pitfalls, and experience it as the truth and reality to the extent that we can rely on that sense of knowing+doing+being.

The thing is, we want to be smart and not vulnerable. We want to be wise and not have any vice. We still want to rely on tales of super heroes and super women whom we want to emulate and when found lacking, lose trust in ourselves and others.

The thing is, lack of trust in the capabilities and wholeness of self and others gives rise to reliance on indexes of control and predictability, which is far from the truth.

The thing is that even the best that we can truly offer to the next generation and what you will be able to offer will be based on our biased tales. With all the knowledge, we still do not know of what will the times be for you. What we do know is that through sharing our tales of trial and error, like our ancestors did, we encourage you to learn to discover your truth.

Celebrate the truth of who you are.

Choose a life that is life-giving.

I hope and pray for all of us to endeavour to truly understand and appreciate the core of our selves, and to see the core human goodness in every other as a constant practice. I trust us. I trust you. I invite you to enjoy Part 6 and transform to BE THE BEST YOU.

Tremblingly,

Your Grandma

PS: So, my lovely grandchildren, what are your stories of transformation as your *Practice of Satsang,* in your times?

A LIFE THAT IS LIFE-GIVING

Diana Jean Reyes

April 22, 2014

A life that is life-giving is filled with Earth
Rooted in Love
Centered in a higher purpose
Unwavering in your belief and acceptance of your own beauty and majesty
…Just like the Great Mountains

Nurturing and generous to all beings
Resilient in the cycles of birth, death and rebirth
Ever-changing, constantly evolving
…Just like Mother Earth

A life that is life-giving is filled with Water
Fully trusting in the flow of life
Unafraid of authenticity and vulnerability
Courageous in self-expression
…Just like the Raging Rivers

Loving, forgiving and compassionate…and that includes with yourself;
Open to feeling the depths of all emotions…yes all of it…
Yet in your heart peace resides, resting in the knowing that "this, too, shall pass"
…Just like the Silent Streams

A life that is life-giving is filled with Air
Everyday filled with a sense of wonder and awe for what life blows your way
Knowing that ideas, inspiration and imagination abound;
Not focused on problems and drama, but rather open to new
perspectives, new horizons and new possibilities
…Just like the vast and clear Blue Sky

Always love in action, even if others may not see
Embracing All as One and One as All
Dancing, moving…uninhibited and free
…Just like the magical Four Winds

A life that is life-giving is filled with Fire
Alive with passion and power
Simultaneously sensual and spiritual
An agent of transformation, within and without
…Just like the burning Sacred Fire

Filled with warmth, joy and laughter like the Rays of Sunshine
Never losing hope and faith, like the Flames of a Candle in a dark room;
Yet gracious in letting go and goodbyes, like the
Sunset heralding the end of the day
Most of all, shining your Light ever so brightly in the best way you
know how - and in doing so, allowing others to do the same
…Just like the Stars in the Heavens

Now, it is time for Practice.
You may create your own or experiment with one I suggest below.

Practice
(T)

To become aware of and take some action when you experience Truth-ache!

- Explore all that is possible to become aware of your truths in life.
- Notice if they are inconsistent. Let them be.
- Allow yourself to feel the pain of the truth-ache which may show up as a numbness, knowing that things are not working in a relationship or area of life, emptiness, lies and dissatisfaction in the inner world.
- Listen to your voice of the soul and take the first courageous step to address the truth-ache

PS: If you believe in the truth-fairy-godmother, trust her to guide you. Do not let the outer world's structures, logic and beliefs uproot you from your truth.

PART
6

Practice of *Satsang* with the Core of Oneself

Unveil self-soul-magnificence ~

~ Letters to my grandchildren ~

My dear little ones, out of the many words you will learn starting with the alphabet 'U', I have a few fundamental ones to share. In addition to 'Umbrella' or 'Uncle', words that helped me to understand the world, the outer world, I was curious to gain access to the mysterious inner world that exists within us. The secret to peace, happiness and fulfillment lies in there. Our inner world determines how we respond to the outer world - people, places and perspectives. Practicing the essence of the few fundamental words below has been life-giving, nourishing and key to expanding possibilities for me

As you grow each day into beautiful beings, I invite you to experiment, play and discover the essence of these words in your life. As you master the game, you will get clues to master your life and create your own future that is meaningful, day-by-day. The key is to choose wisely and practice consciously. Remember, whatever you practice; consciously, sub-consciously, or unconsciously, right or wrong, it grows stronger. So, what do you choose?

U for 'Understanding'

- When are times when you have felt you truly understood yourself; your true intentions, your conflicting parts, your wholeness?
- What do you practice to accept and act from that inner knowing?

U for 'Uniqueness'

- What is your unique gift that you bring to this world?
- What do you practice to grow, sustain that inner uniqueness?

U for 'Universe' and 'Unity'

- What is your role in the universe – of your inner world and outer world?
- What do practice to unite all your feelings, thoughts and feel complete?

Other words, still starting with 'U', also served me but only for short-term. Practice of the essence of these words fed my ego and exhausted me in the long-term as I found them to be life-depleting;

U for 'Uselessness', 'Uptightness' and 'Ugly'.

Practice of *Satsang* with the Core of Oneself – A Story

Unveil self-soul-magnificence ~

(Now from this part of the book,
I invite you as your *Practice of Satsang* with Core of Your Self, in your times,
to write stories of your own moments of magnificence,
freedom, courage and dignity.
Think of a time/s
when you saw, got in touch and courageously
unveiled your own magnificence.
You believed in yourself and stepped out of your
limiting thoughts, emotions, and boundaries.)

"I follow my heart. I love myself, life and Life. Today is where it's at and here is where I want to be. I can change, I am change, change is everything."

-Mischa Oliver Altmann (2014)
-(Global Change maker from Austria, Insightful fool)

"Treasure all your experience-good or bad-as they add up to your wisdom and learning. Go with curiosity to explore every day!"

-Melinda Varfi (2014)
-(Global Change maker from Hungary, Soulful Nurturer)

Now, it is time for Practice.
You may create your own or experiment with one I suggest below.

Practice
(U)

To unveil your own self-magnificence through courage, mindfulness and dignity.

Pick any of the below to pay attention to, at any time of the day or night, in any form – be it a self-dialogue, a conversation with another, sitting in silence with it, writing, or any other form of expression for exploration.

- Who are You?
    - o Who are you when you are rested, when things are going as you had planned and when you are meeting with success?
    - o Who are you when you are exhausted, when things are not going as you had planned and when you are meeting with failure?
    - o Who are you when you have paradoxical thoughts and emotions? Who are you when you accept your wholeness, as natural of having both of whatever it is that you judge to be good/bad?

- You may say to yourself, for example, 'I accept my soul magnificence and choose to act in the best way possible, that I know of now.'

PS: Once you own your magnificence, you see the magnificence in others too, even in their imperfections. Look out for it. The world turns into a magnificent space.

Vintage health and self-care ~

~ Letters to my grandchildren ~

My dear little ones, out of the many words you will learn starting with the alphabet 'V', I have a few fundamental ones to share. In addition to 'Van' or 'Vase', words that helped me to understand the world, the outer world, I was curious to gain access to the mysterious inner world that exists within us. The secret to peace, happiness and fulfillment lies in there. Our inner world determines how we respond to the outer world - people, places and perspectives. Practicing the essence of the few fundamental words below has been life-giving, nourishing and key to expanding possibilities for me.

As you grow each day into beautiful beings, I invite you to experiment, play and discover the essence of these words in your life. As you master the game, you will get clues to master your life and create your own future that is meaningful, day-by-day. The key is to choose wisely and practice consciously. Remember, whatever you practice; consciously, sub-consciously, or unconsciously, right or wrong, it grows stronger. So, what do you choose?

V for 'Vulnerability'

- What is your comfort in being, accepting and showing vulnerability?
- Why might vulnerability allow true compassion for others?

V for 'Validation'

- What do you validate yourself for? Do you look for external and/or internal validation?
- Why might validation allow true connection with others?

V for 'Value and Self - Worth'

- What do you value your life for?
- What are you learning about self-respect, self-worth and self-dignity?

Other words, still starting with 'V', also served me but only for short-term. Practice of the essence of these words fed my ego and exhausted me in the long-term as I found them to be life-depleting;

V for 'Vehemence', 'Vanity' and 'Vulgarity'.

Practice of *Satsang* with the Core of Oneself – A Story

Vintage health and self-care ~

(What is your story of vintage secrets for physical, mental and soulful health and self-care?)

"Good health is an inevitable necessity for quality life".

-Sarat Kumar Jain (2013)
(61 years old, Entrepreneur,
one of my uncles and rare adults in his age,
whom I witnessed as balancing discipline for health
with curiosity and flexibility.)

Now, it is time for Practice.
You may create your own or experiment with one I suggest below.

Practice
(V)

To discover, explore, create, affirm and practice that which is nourishing for health.

- Observe your beliefs of what does good health mean to you. Is it purely physical or do you understand your entire system?
- Observe your practices, or lack there of, to sustain good health.
- Where did you learn your first habits for good health? Test to see if they are sound or are they dependent on medicines and methods that are not self-reliant?
- Take out some time for yourself to read, learn and integrate practices, sports, meditation and self-care.

P.S. Make it a discipline.

Walking butterfly ~

~ Letters to my grandchildren ~

My dear little ones, out of the many words you will learn starting with the alphabet 'W', I have a few fundamental ones to share. In addition to 'Watch' or 'Water', words that helped me to understand the world, the outer world, I was curious to gain access to the mysterious inner world that exists within us. The secret to peace, happiness and fulfillment lies in there. Our inner world determines how we respond to the outer world - people, places and perspectives. Practicing the essence of the few fundamental words below has been life-giving, nourishing and key to expanding possibilities for me.

As you grow each day into beautiful beings, I invite you to experiment, play and discover the essence of these words in your life. As you master the game, you will get clues to master your life and create your own future that is meaningful, day-by-day. The key is to choose wisely and practice consciously. Remember, whatever you practice; consciously, sub-consciously, or unconsciously, right or wrong, it grows stronger. So, what do you choose?

W for 'Warm' and 'Welcoming'

- Who are You?
- What/who do you surrender to?

W for 'Wild'

- What is your natural self in relation with the environment?
- What do you do to unleash your energy and passion for what you truly care about?

W for 'Worthwhile'

- What is worthy of your commitment?
- What is worthwhile to give everything for?

Other words, still starting with 'W', also served me but only for short-term. Practice of the essence of these words fed my ego and exhausted me in the long-term as I found them to be life-depleting;

W for 'Wasteful', 'Wicked' and 'Whiny'.

Practice of *Satsang* with the Core of Oneself – A Story

Walking butterfly ~

(What is your story of transformation in yourself
like from a caterpillar to a butterfly?
What magic do you believe in pursuing to fly and
enable others in the ecosystem too?)

"I am stressed with this purpose of life. What if there is no purpose in life, and we are born simply to be, and to live each day authentically and with awareness."

-Meenakshi Swarup (2014)
(Healer, Law of Attraction Entrepreneur,
who changed her career path to live her dreams
and help others attain theirs too.)

Now, it is time for Practice.
You may create your own or experiment with one I suggest below.

Practice
(W)

To be a witness of your own natural transformation as guided by your wise self.

- What is a metaphor from nature that you resonate with at the moment?
    o Is it a mountain? Is it a river? Is it a hot spring? Is it a maple tree, a melting glacier, a spider or perhaps a snow leopard?
    o Pick one and experiment living a week, for instance, true to your chosen metaphor – How would a mountain respond to challenges at work, in relationships, to financial graphs, to gains and to losses?
    o Read up on your chosen metaphor to seek the true nature of the natural element and check how does it fit with your own human nature?
    o What are you surprised by, touched by?
- What do you truly care about in nature? Commit to nurturing and attending to nature, be it a plant, a pet, to keep a park, river or lake clean – whatever it is that you can create in your circle of influence. Invite family and friends to commit to a part that they care about too.
- Walk in nature – Commit to connecting with nature on a regular basis.
- Watch yourself watching the world. You are part of it and if you take care of yourself to live fully, you are doing your part.

P.S. Look out for wonder in the transformation and unfolding of lessons learnt from nature – that which is within you and that which is outside too.

X-ray intentions ~

~ Letters to my grandchildren ~

My dear little ones, out of the many words you will learn starting with the alphabet 'X', I have a few fundamental ones to share. In addition to 'Xerox' or 'Xylophone', words that helped me to understand the world, the outer world, I was curious to gain access to the mysterious inner world that exists within us. The secret to peace, happiness and fulfillment lies in there. Our inner world determines how we respond to the outer world - people, places and perspectives. Practicing the essence of the few fundamental words below has been life-giving, nourishing and key to expanding possibilities for me.

As you grow each day into beautiful beings, I invite you to experiment, play and discover the essence of these words in your life. As you master the game, you will get clues to master your life and create your own future that is meaningful, day-by-day. The key is to choose wisely and practice consciously. Remember, whatever you practice; consciously, sub-consciously, or unconsciously, right or wrong, it grows stronger. So, what do you choose?

X for 'Xoxo'

- What new ways of communication has the 21st century surfaced that is helpful?
- Do you truly mean and feel the emotions you express in abbreviations?

Other words, still starting with 'X', also served me but only for short-term. Practice of the essence of these words fed my ego and exhausted me in the long-term as I found them to be life-depleting;

X for 'Xenophobic'and 'X'd out'.

Practice of *Satsang* with the Core of Oneself – A Story

X-ray intentions ~

(What is your story of x-raying your intentions from
your own consciousness and sub-consciousness?)

"Indulgence is a necessity.
Allow yourself to completely indulge in your experiences/adventures."

-Dipesh Punjabi (2013)
-(Entrepreneur,
whom I have seen commit toall that he believed in,
be it business, travel, hobbies, spiritual pursuit, health
and live life to the fullest.)

Now, it is time for Practice.
You may create your own or experiment with one I suggest below.

Practice
(X)

To x-ray self thoughts, emotions and actions for what serves in your life.

- Learn to differentiate between diverse threads of your thoughts and emotions; intentions, dreams, desires, fears, learned behaviours/habits, questions, curiosity...
- Allow yourself to listen to all your positive and negative thoughts. Sit with all the thoughts and emotions without judgment as you would with a crying or smiling infant. Accept every part (both light and shadow sides) without attachment and judgment as it is part of your truth, even if it is for a moment. Remember, however, that you are more than the sum of all these parts.
- Ask each of them, 'what is the message I am to receive from you?'
- You may self-inquire, 'what happened before that thought and/or emotion? And what happened prior to that? And prior to that – till you reach its roots or an insight or implication for yourself.'
- Understand and appreciate yourself. Observe, think, learn and act wisely from the center of your purpose.

- Learn to unlearn and let go of what does not serve.
- Enjoy the silence and the peace.
- Unlearn to learn and welcome that which serves.

P.S. Sharpen your inner world's dissecting tools.

Yin-Yang dance ~

~ Letters to my grandchildren ~

My dear little ones, out of the many words you will learn starting with the alphabet 'Y', I have a few fundamental ones to share. In addition to 'Yacht' or 'Yahoo', words that helped me to understand the world, the outer world, I was curious to gain access to the mysterious inner world that exists within us. The secret to peace, happiness and fulfillment lies in there. Our inner world determines how we respond to the outer world - people, places and perspectives. Practicing the essence of the few fundamental words below has been life-giving, nourishing and key to expanding possibilities for me.

As you grow each day into beautiful beings, I invite you to experiment, play and discover the essence of these words in your life. As you master the game, you will get clues to master your life and create your own future that is meaningful, day-by-day. The key is to choose wisely and practice consciously. Remember, whatever you practice; consciously, sub-consciously, or unconsciously, right or wrong, it grows stronger. So, what do you choose?

Y for 'Youthful'

- How do you keep your heart young and free, no matter what age you maybe?
- What are you learning from the youth?

Y for 'Yearning'

- What is your heart telling you?
- Why might it be important to attune yourself to others' hearts?

Y for 'Yielding'

- What are you ready to let go of? What are you holding on to?
- How humble are you as you interact with the world?

Other words, still starting with 'Y', also served me but only for short-term. Practice of the essence of these words fed my ego and exhausted me in the long-term as I found them to be life-depleting;

Y for feeling 'Yucky' and 'Yellow'.

Practice of *Satsang* with the Core of Oneself – A Story

Yin-Yang dance ~

(What is your story of balancing your own masculinity and femininity energy, irrespective of your gender and the gender construction by culture?)

"Let go to let come."
Many teachers remind me of this eternal truth.

Now, it is time for Practice.
You may create your own or experiment with one I suggest below.

Practice
(Y)

To be in flow.

- Select three to five values that are meaningful for you.
- Do NOT speak of those values or the meaning with anyone. Shh, it is your secret!
- See who are you with your family, friends, fellow-travelers, clients, colleagues, community and strangers walking, talking and living those values in your day-to-day family and business life.
- Notice when you are not living your life by your own values. Hug yourself for your awareness and attempt to live it in the next moment, when you feel ready.
- Do you need to change the values or the meaning they held for you? What brings you peace and contentment?
- Remember, you can be in delicious flow in your inner world in any given moment. Observe how the outer world changes as per the flow of your inner world. Practice consciously.

P.S. Enjoy your inner yin-yang dance, the ups, the downs and the moments.

Zzz...zz..z. ~

~ Letters to my grandchildren ~

My dear little ones, out of the many words you will learn starting with the alphabet 'Z', I have a few fundamental ones to share. In addition to 'Zebra' or 'Zinc', words that helped me to understand the world, the outer world, I was curious to gain access to the mysterious inner world that exists within us. The secret to peace, happiness and fulfillment lies in there. Our inner world determines how we respond to the outer world - people, places and perspectives. Practicing the essence of the few fundamental words below has been life-giving, nourishing and key to expanding possibilities for me.

As you grow each day into beautiful beings, I invite you to experiment, play and discover the essence of these words in your life. As you master the game, you will get clues to master your life and create your own future that is meaningful, day-by-day. The key is to choose wisely and practice consciously. Remember, whatever you practice; consciously, sub-consciously, or unconsciously, right or wrong, it grows stronger. So, what do you choose?

Z for 'Zest'

- What makes you zestful?
- What do you do to make others feel alive and zestful?

Z for 'Zen'

- What is Zen for you?
- What do you practice to cultivate this consciousness?

Z for 'Zero'

- What does nothingness mean to you?
- How do you make something out of nothingness and when?

Other words, still starting with 'Z', also served me but only for short-term. Practice of the essence of these words fed my ego and exhausted me in the long-term as I found them to be life-depleting; Z for 'Zombie-like-acts' and feeling 'Zapped'.

Practice of *Satsang* with the Core of Oneself – A Story

Zzz…zz..z. ~

(There is a time to read, a time to reflect, a time to write, a time to create, a time to share, a time to practice, a time to play, a time to rest and a time to Zzz…zz..z.)

"Before the eternal zzz, embraces us, we are called to live with love, that's it. Celebrating the sacred ever-expanding gift of consciousness."

-Natasha Dalmia (2013)
-(Soul in various roles)

Now, it is time for Practice.
You may create your own or experiment with one I suggest below.

Practice
(Z)

To Zzz..zz..z.

- Notice what keeps you from sleeping and what brings you good, deep, restful and rejuvenating sleep.
- Practice taking out time to sleep consciously for the allotted amount of time that you need.
- Keep a dream journal next to you if you wish to write your dreams in the first few moments of waking up. Make a request to your own consciousness to interpret and learn well from your dreams.
- Thank your sub-conscious lovingly as it integrates, heals and works while you rest your consciousness.

P.S. Enjoy the precious snatches of zzz (Ask anyone who cannot fall asleep, sometimes even with medicines, how priceless is the value of a good sleep?!!)

Thank You for holding the space for my letters to the future,
learning from the past,
living in the perfect present.